DEWI'

Twelve landmarks are gi
Five crosses indicate those for w
text; the sixth is the water of the ri

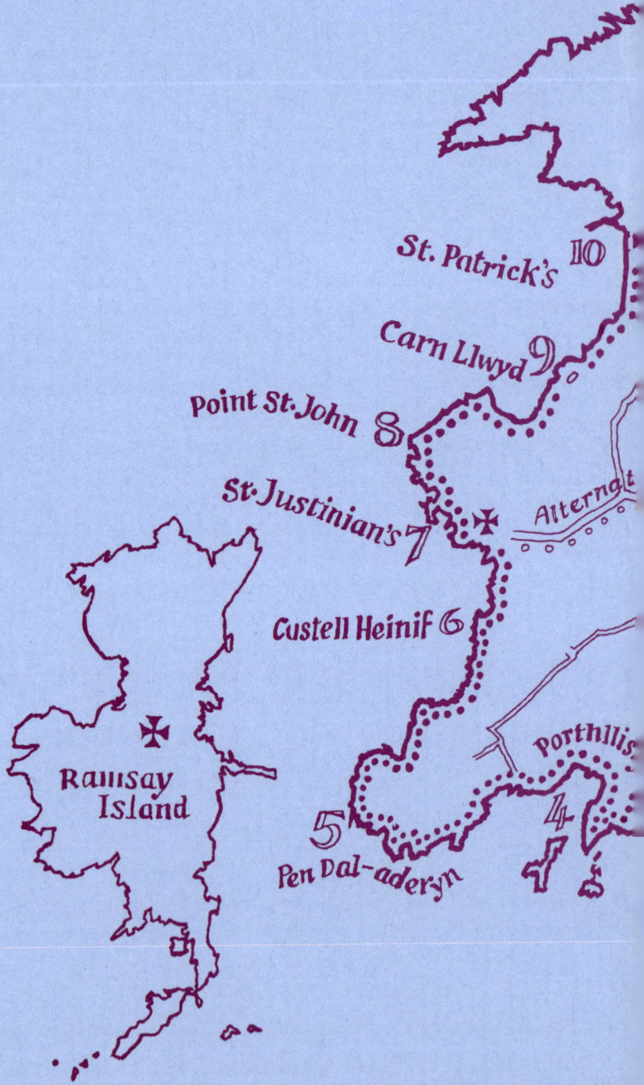

LAND

…s suggested stations. …there are prayers in the …and the sea.

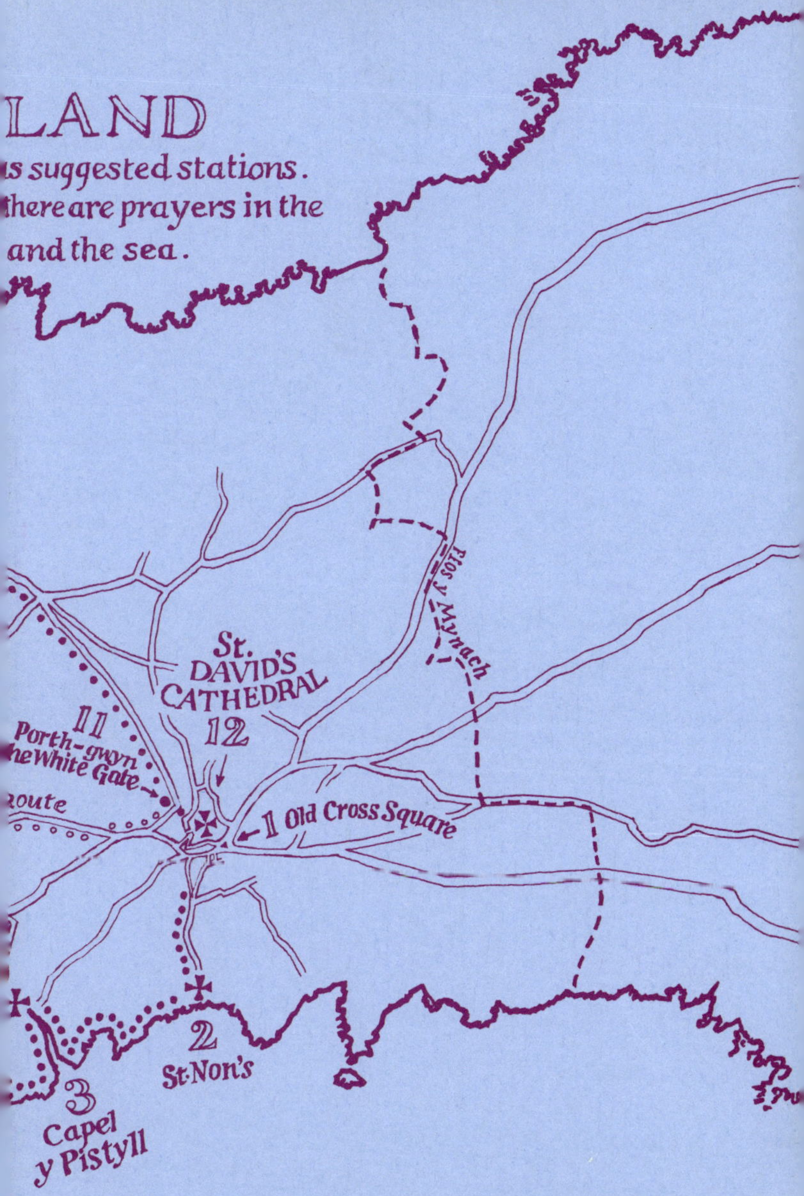

A PILGRIM'S MANUAL

A PILGRIM'S MANUAL

St. David's

compiled by Brian Brendan O'Malley

with a foreword by A. M. Allchin
and wood engravings by Simon Brett

And so we came to the end of the world
where the patron saint of Wales sleeps by the Western sea
Francis Kilvert, October 1871

PAULINUS PRESS
1985

Published by
PAULINUS PRESS
12 Blowhorn Street
Marlborough, Wilts. SN8 1BT
England

This Manual is dedicated to
WILLIAM MORRIS
Verger
a long and faithful servant
to the Cathedral of Saint David.

British Library Cataloguing in Publication data

A Pilgrim's Manual: Saint David's.
1. Christian pilgrims and pilgrimages—Wales
—Dyfed—Prayer-books and devotions
I. O'Malley, Brian Brendan
248.4'63'0942962 BV5067

ISBN 0 907740 13 8
ISBN 0 907740 12 X Pbk

Set in 10/11 pt. Perpetua
and printed in Wales
at the Gomer Press, Llandysul, Dyfed.

CONTENTS

FOREWORD

It is remarkable and wonderfully hopeful thing that in the last thirty or forty years many of the ancient holy places of our island of Britain, Prydein Fawr, have been re-asserting themselves in ways that no-one could have forseen. Iona and Walsingham, Glastonbury and Lindisfarn, Canterbury and Bardsey, to mention only a few, have revealed themselves once again as places of life-giving peace, of a healing presence. After centuries of neglect and indifference such places are coming to be known and loved areas. The prayers of the Saints are once more invoked and appreciated. Men and women who would never have expected to become pilgrims have found themselves drawn to such places, and have found in them not some devotional luxury, but a clarity and vision which are necessary for any truly human life.

One of the greatest poets of our time has spoken about the conditions of a true pilgrimage in words that are not easily forgotten.

> You are not here to verify,
> Instruct yourself, or inform curiosity
> Or carry report. You are here to kneel
> Where prayer has been valid. And prayer is more
> Than an order of words, the conscious occupation
> Of the praying mind, or the sound of the voice praying.
> And what the dead had no speech for, when living,
> They can tell you, being dead: the communication
> Of the dead is tongued with fire beyond the language of
> the living.

You are here to kneel. The physical act is important, just as the physical place is important. There is something sacramental about holy places. The fact that in them we find God near does not mean that all other places are empty of God's presence and power. God's wisdom and love are at work throughout his creation. But places which have been centres of prayer, that is centres of the encounter between God and man, between earth and heaven, retain a particular kind of openness. Here the Kingdom of Heaven draws very close.

Among all such places St. David's has a very special place. One of the great centres of Celtic Christendom, nature and grace have come together to make of it a particularly memorable spot. The hidden presence of the first Christian centuries, the prayers of Saint David himself and his many companions, the devotion of generations of people known and unknown who have come to worship here, all these things have marked out this place with a quality all its own.

The prayers and praises which have been gathered into this remarkable collection will allow many more to enter in to something of the riches of this House of David, this place particularly dear to the people of Wales and to all who honour the ancient British tongue, but also beloved by those of other parts of Britain and Ireland and of many from beyond these shores. In a way almost without parallel, David has remained a living presence for Christians of many different traditions through the centuriess. May his prayers be powerful now to bring us all together in the unity which is our Lord's will and prayer for us.

A. M. Allchin

Caergaint. Dydd Gwyl yr Ystwyll. 1985.

FROM THE BISHOP OF ST. DAVID'S

Life is a pilgrimage and to be a Christian is to be a pilgrim. For a thousand years pilgrims have come to St. Davids and today the theme of pilgrimage is once again important. Every year thousands of pilgrims visit our beautiful cathedral to see and touch the holy; to satisfy man's universal need and desire to worship God, to adore the beautiful and to seek the Truth. This Pilgrim's Manual has grown from the experience of the Revd. Brendan O'Malley who is the chaplain of the cathedral and has conducted innumerable groups of pilgrims around the shrine of our patron saint and the holy places that surround it. Through his interest in Celtic spirituality he has provided us with an anthology of prayers, poems and hymns. I am delighted to commend this book to all who visit St. Davids and I hope that it will enrich and deepen their spiritual life.

George St. Davids

PREFACE

Deep peace of the running wave to you
Deep peace of the flowing air to you
Deep peace of the quiet earth to you
Deep peace of the shining stars to you
Deep peace of the Son of Peace to you.

The idea for a Pilgrim's Manual, a companion to prayer which can always be *at hand,* came to me when leading groups of pilgrims around Dewisland and thence to the Cathedral shrine of Saint David. Some people come to Saint David's *as* pilgrims, some as visitors; but many are touched by the spirit of the place to want to savour the mystery of the incarnation as experienced by the early Celtic saints. What could be more natural when hearing the larks singing, watching the sun struggling through the mist over St. Bride's Bay or visiting some holy well, than to have thoughts that tend to prayer and to feel the need for a manual to collect one's prayer together and to enable one to practice the presence of God and to see Him in everything as they did?

The Celtic saints were imbued with the mysterious reality of the continuing presence of God, His immanent presence in the world, and therefore with the Incarnational nature of all creation. In the way they recognised this mystery, their world view was closer to our own than that of many of the intervening centuries with their more intellectual and doctrinal formulations. They had a deep and abiding love of Holy Writ, evidenced in the beautifully illuminated texts of the period and they cultivated the love of learning and of piety; but, more important, to a rural people, very close to nature, very 'down to earth' and dwelling in a sacral environment, every well-spring, wood and stone took on a mystical significance. No doubt, this proceeded from their pagan past, but that was transformed, its numinous properties spiritualised, by Christian prayer. The Scottish Gaelic language has a phrase "Are you going to church?" which, when literally translated, says "Are you going to the stones?".The awareness of the whole world as Incarnational was linked in to a tremendous 'spirit of place'. Saint David's *locates* for us this long and deep, spiritual and cultural tradition. It is older than Iona, Lindisfarne or Canterbury as a Christian settlement; and I think it is more impressive

The manual is both a prayer book and an anthology, intended for private devotion or for liturgical use on pilgrimages. The style of the prayers is kept in the classical language in which they were written; they may be best appreciated when enunciated and sounded slowly, digested meditatively, so as to become 'organic praise', the prayer of the whole person.

The form of the first half of the book should be clear from the Contents page: the Itinerarium or Itinerary, the blessing of travellers before a journey; then, the series of gradual psalms, the ancient songs sung by the Israelites on their way to the Temple in Jerusalem, with alternative prayers taken from old texts for use at the end of each 'station'. A 'station', as on the railways, is just a stopping place, whether one stops for tea or for thought; often we want to sit down and meditate when on pilgrimage. How you use the book will depend on how many stops or 'stations' are made on the way to St. David's or around its countryside; and the formality or informality of its use on company and circumstance. A greeting, a psalm, the Our Father, responses, collect and the versicle "Let us go forth in peace" may be as well read on your own as aloud with a group who are 'making the pilgrimage' together. Stations are therefore suggested for the Dewisland Walk, including the beautiful Eastern Orthodox rite of the Blessing of the Waters in an adapted, shorter form for liturgy and meditation; and the idea is that the gradual psalms and some of the poetry in the second part of the book be used when sitting and resting on the way, so that the two parts, though separated for clarity, may flow together in the practice of prayer. Stations are given for arrival at the Cathedral and a further series follows commencing with the renewal of Baptismal vows at the font, continuing with a visit to the shrine of Saint David and culminating at the Chapel of the Blessed Sacrament. It is perhaps more in harmony with the place than going round with a guide book in your hand.

I would like to thank Morwenna, my wife, for her patience in typing the early notes; and Joanne, my sister-in-law, for the drafting of the typescript; and Donald Moore and Dr. Geraint Gruffydd of the National Library of Wales for their invaluable advice. I am also deeply indebted to Catrin Stevens of Caslllwchwr for her assistance in the understanding of the ancient Welsh texts.

Brendan O'Malley

A LITURGY
FOR PILGRIMS

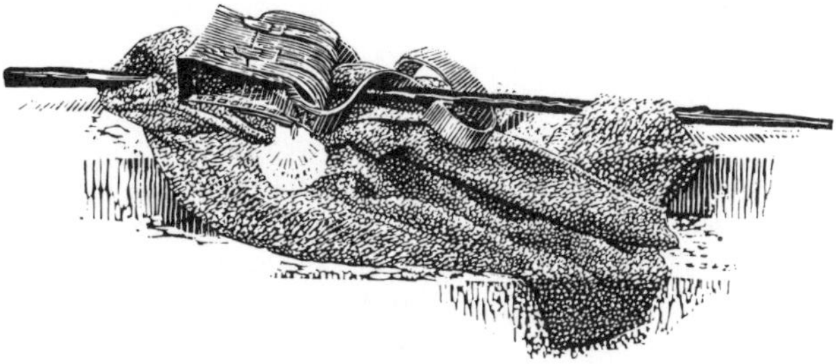

SETTING OUT

Give me my scallop shell of quiet,
My staff of faith to walk upon,
My scrip of joy, immortal diet,
My bottle of salvation,
My gown of glory, hope's true gage,
And thus I'll take my pilgrimage.
Sir Walter Raleigh

The Consecration of Pilgrims

During the early life of the Church, the pilgrimage came into vogue as a physical means of obtaining the spiritual expiation of sin through self-imposed exile, financial penance and long journeys to the shrine of a holy person who had been deeply imbued with the Holy Spirit; and the pilgrimage would begin from the person's own church and with the blessing of the Church.

It was deemed indispensable that the pilgrims first confessed all their sins. After this they lay prostrate before the altar. Particular prayers and psalms were said over them, at the end of which the pilgrims arose and the priest consecrated their scrips (satchels) and staves. He sprinkled holy water on the scrips and staves and placed the scrip around the neck of the pilgrim, with further prayers. Then he gave him the staff, with similar prayers. If any of the pilgrims were going to Jerusalem, their garments were in readiness, marked with the cross, and the crosses were consecrated and holy water sprinkled over them. The garments and crosses were then delivered to the pilgrims, accompanied again by appropriate prayers. The service concluded with the Mass, *De Iter Agentibus.*

Offerings were given for the consecration of the scrip. In *The Penitential of Theodore* it is said 'In the aforesaid Church the Priest is accustomed to consecrate the Scrip and Staves of the Pilgrims, and receive 1d. from the oblation.'

Elsewhere it appears, concerning Jerusalem Pilgrims, that immediately after the Sermon preached on the occasion, the cross was sewn upon the shoulders, and at least placed there by the Bishop; to affix the cross was a privilege of that order only.

Even kings assumed the scrip and staff. King Richard I at Tours, in sign of his immediately undertaking the pilgrimage to the Holy Land, received the scrip and staff.

The arms of the pilgrims were also consecrated; and pilgrims were licenced and led out in procession from the parish when going to Jerusalem, Rome or St. James (Sant Iago) or St. David's, with the cross, holy water and procession.

The Pilgrims' Badge—The Scallop Shell

Although in the Middle Ages the scallop was used as a design for the ornamentation of buildings, furniture, coffins, coins, its most famous use was as a pilgrims' badge, which derived from its connection with the shrine of St. James of Compostela. St. James the Greater, one of Christ's apostles, was the evangelist of Spain who on returning to Jerusalem was beheaded by Herod Agrippa. He was buried at Jerusalem, but the Spanish tradition claims that his remains were translated to Galicia and later to Compostella, where his shrine became a famous place of pilgrimage. Special travel booklets were published to assist the pilgrim travellers and the custom of giving pilgrimage souvenirs grew here as a result of an enterprising salesman. Piles of empty scallop shells, brought in sixteen miles from the sea for food purposes, were sold to pilgrims and rapidly became the symbol of pilgrimage.

Soon the scallop shell design appeared on statues of St. James together with the pilgrim hat. It appeared on the stained glass windows of cathedrals and on the heraldry of noble families who had been on crusade or pilgrimage to Jerusalem, Rome or Compostella. Mystical symbols appealed to the medieval eye and so the scallop symbol is very often depicted, with one or two slits for hanging round the pilgrim's neck or for fixing to the neck-strap of the crusader's horse to show that the knight had been to war in search of the Holy Grail, the cup traditionally thought to have been used by Jesus Christ at the Last Supper.

The custom of blessing the scallop shell, the pilgrim badge, is still in force today, that the King of Pilgrims may guide and protect by His Spirit those who wear and carry them as they journey to their Heavenly Home.

The Saint David's Pilgrims' Badge is the Sunset Shell, to be found on the beaches in the Dewisland area. When you look towards the sun all shadows fall behind you and when you look to The Son of God 'The Way' lies before you.

THE ITINERARY

The Blessing of those beginning a journey

May the road rise to meet you.
May the wind be always at your back.
May the sun shine warm upon your face, the rains fall soft upon your fields and, until we meet again,
May God hold you in the palm of his hand.

v. The Lord be with you.
r. And also with you.

Let us listen to the Gospel of the Lord.

Reading Luke 10: 23-37

And behold, a lawyer stood up to put him to the test, saying, 'Teacher, what shall I do to inherit eternal life?' He said to him, 'What is written in the law? How do you read?' And he answered, 'You shall love the Lord your God with all your heart, and with all your soul, and with all your strength, and with all your mind; and your neighbour as yourself.' And he said to him, 'You have answered right; do this, and you will live.'

But he, desiring to justify himself, said to Jesus, 'And who is my neighbour?' Jesus replied, 'A man was going down from Jerusalem to Jericho, and he fell among robbers, who stripped him and beat him, and departed, leaving him half dead. Now by chance a priest was going down that road; and when he saw him he passed by on the other side. So likewise a Levite, when he came to the place and saw him, passed by on the other side. But a Samaritan, as he journeyed, came to where he was; and when he saw him, he had compassion, and went to him and bound up his wounds, pouring on oil and wine; then he set him on his own beast and brought him to an inn, and took care of him. And the next day he took out two denarii and gave them to the innkeeper, saying, "Take care of him: and whatever more you spend, I will repay you when I come back." Which of these three, do you think, proved neighbour to the man who fell among the robbers?' He said, 'The one who showed mercy on him.' And Jesus said to him, 'Go and do likewise.'

Responsorial Psalm

R. You will show me the path of life.

1. Preserve me, God, I take refuge in you.
I say to the Lord: 'You are my God.'
O Lord, it is you who are my portion and cup,
it is you yourself who are my prize. R.

2. I will bless the Lord who gives me counsel,
who even at night directs my heart.
I keep the Lord ever in my sight, since he is
at my right hand, I shall stand firm. R.

3. And so my heart rejoices, my soul is glad;
even my body shall rest in safety.
For you will not lead my soul among the
dead, nor let your beloved know decay. R.

4. You will show me the path of life,
the fullness of joy in your presence,
at your right hand happiness for ever. R.

The Blessing of the Pilgrim Badges

O, Almighty God, who hath called these thy servants to take their part in this Pilgrimage, we beseech Thee to bless and sanctify these shells, and to grant that they who shall wear them, being filled with humility, penitence and devotion, may go forth in peace and attain their heart's desire, and that when life's Pilgrimage is over, they may by Thy grace, rest in the Heavenly Country; through Jesus Christ our Lord. **Amen.**

The Pilgrim Badges are then given to the Pilgrims

Alternative Blessing

Be these shells blessed by the King of Pilgrims that all who shall carry them may be guided and protected by His Spirit as they journey to their Heavenly Home: in the Name of the Father and of the Son and of the Holy Spirit. **Amen.**

The Benedictus Luke 1: 68

Blessed be the Lord God of Israel: for he hath visited and redeemed his people;
And hath raised up a mighty salvation for us: in the house of his servant David;
As he spake by the mouth of his holy prophets: which have been since the world began;
That we should be saved from our enemies: and from the hands of all that hate us:
To perform the mercy promised to our forefathers: and to remember his holy covenant;
To perform the oath: which he swore to our forefather Abraham;
That we being delivered out of the hands of our enemies: might serve him without fear;
In holiness and righteousness before him: all the days of our life;
And thou, child, shalt be called the Prophet of the Highest: for thou shalt go before the face of the Lord to prepare his ways;

To give knowledge of salvation unto his people: for the remission of their sins;
Through the tender mercy of our God: whereby the day-spring from on high hath visited us;
To give light to them that sit in darkness, and in the shadow of death: and to guide our feet into the way of peace.
Glory be to the Father, and to the Son: and to the Holy Spirit;
As it was in the beginning, is now, and ever shall be: world without end. Amen.

Let us pray

Heavenly Father, protector of all who trust in you, you led your people in safety through the desert and brought them to a land of plenty. Guide these your faithful people who begin their journey today. Fill them with your spirit of love. Preserve them from all harm, and bring them in safety to their destination. We ask this through Christ our Lord.

The priest holds his right hand over the persons who are about to begin their journey, and says:

May our Lord Jesus Christ be with you to defend you, within you to keep you, before you to lead you, behind you to guard you, above you to bless you. We ask this of Him who lives and reigns with the Father and the Holy Spirit for ever and ever. **Amen.**

An Alternative Gaelic Blessing

Be the great God between thy two shoulders
To protect thee in thy going and in thy coming.
Be the Son of Mary Virgin near thine heart,
And be the perfect Spirit upon thee pouring—
Oh, the perfect Spirit upon thee pouring.

ON THE JOURNEY

To treat a journey as a pilgrimage is to make it a symbolic act whereby we recognise the transitory nature of our life on earth and that it has a greater goal beyond itself; and whereby we pledge in faith that it is a journey towards God.

Pilgrims come to St. David's from afar; for them the Songs of the Road below are given. Others may like to enter the spirit of the pilgrim by taking the Dewisland walk, six stations for which are given on p. 21-45; for them, the Songs may provide alternative or additional material for prayer.

The 'Gradual' Psalms or 'Songs of Ascents' were songs for those going *up to* Jerusalem. Within the Book of Psalms, they are a ready-made handbook of devotions for travellers; they may be individualised and spiritualised and used as a guide by the believing pilgrim as he marches each day towards the heavenly city.

Those with a Psalter will find many other psalms that are appropriate to the landscape of St. David's; a selection is listed on p. 17. 'Sentences' are given to assist the saying of the psalms; any of them may be selected and recited before the chosen psalm. The prayers, responses and concluding prayers that are customary after the psalm(s) are given on pp. 18-20. Eastern Orthodox pilgrims' prayers will be found on p. 157. On arriving at a 'station', therefore the pilgrim(s) might recite a four-part sequence:

- ☐ one of the sentences (pp. 9, 10)
- ☐ one of the psalms (or more, at choice) with the Glory be to the Father after each. (pp. 10-17).
- ☐ the Lord have mercy, Our Father and one or more of the further set of responses (pp. 18, 19).
- ☐ and one of the short Concluding Prayers (pp. 19, 20) with the final versicle and response.

AT THE STATIONS ON THE JOURNEY

The Sentences

1 v. Be thou my Rock and my refuge that thou mayest preserve me:
r. For thou are my strong rock and my castle.

2 v. There is a river, the streams whereof make glad the city of God:
r. The holy dwelling place of the Most Highest.

3 v. O send out thy light and thy truth, that they may lead me:
r. And bring me unto thy holy hill and to thy dwelling.

4 v. Let all the earth fear the Lord:
r. Let them stand in awe of him, all they that dwell in the world.

5 v. Be thou my strong rock and house of defence: that thou mayest save me.
r. For thou art my strong rock and my castle: be thou also my guide and lead me for thy name's sake.

6 v. To-day earth and sea shall share in the joy of the world:
r. And the world is filled with gladness.

7 v. Show me thy ways O Lord:
r. And teach me thy paths.

8 v. Them that are meek shall he guide in right paths: and such as are gentle, them shall he teach his way.
r. All the paths of the Lord are mercy and truth: unto such as keep his covenant and his testimonies.

9 v. Thy word is a lantern unto my feet:
r. And a light unto my path.

10 v. The Lord is righteous in all his ways:
r. And merciful in all his works.

11 v. The Spirit of the Lord has filled the world.
r. God will give strength unto his people; blessed be God.

12 v. The Lord shall be King for evermore.
r. Holiness becometh thine house, O Lord, for ever.

13 v. Show me thy way, O Lord:
r. Lead me forth in thy truth and teach me.

14 v. I have set God always before me:
r. He is on my right hand, therefore I shall not fall.

15 v. Teach me thy way O Lord, that I may walk in Thy truth:
r. O let my heart rejoice in reverence for thy name.

16 v. Blessed are those that are blameless in their lives: and walk in the law of the Lord.
r. Blessed are they that keep his testimonies: and seek him with their whole heart.

17 v. Tremble thou earth at the presence of the Lord: at the presence of the God of Jacob,
r. Who turned the hard rock into pools of water: and the flint-stone into a springing well.

The Gradual Psalms

Psalm 120

1. When I was in trouble I called upon the Lord: and he hearkened unto my calling.
2. Deliver me O Lord from lying lips: and from a deceitful tongue.
3. What shall be done unto thee: and what more shall God add unto thee, O thou deceitful tongue?
4. The sharp arrows of a mighty warrior: with fire that burneth like coals.
5. Woe is me that I dwell in Meshech: and have my habitation among the tents of Kedar.
6. Full long have I had my dwelling: among them that are enemies unto peace.
7. I labour for peace: but when I speak thereof, they make them ready for battle.

Psalm 121

1. I will lift up mine eyes unto the hills: from whence cometh my help?

2. My help cometh from the Lord: who hath made heaven and earth.

3. He will not suffer thy foot to be moved: and he that keepeth thee will not sleep.

4. Behold he that keepeth Israel: shall neither slumber nor sleep.

5. The Lord himself is thy keeper: the Lord upon thy right hand shall give thee shade;

6. The sun shall not strike thee by day: neither shall the moon by night.

7. The Lord shall preserve thee from all evil: yea it is he that shall keep thee safe.

8. The Lord shall preserve thy going out and thy coming in: from this time forth for evermore.

Psalm 122

1. I was glad when they said unto me: 'Let us go to the house of the Lord.'

2. Now our feet are standing: within thy gates O Jerusalem,

3. Jerusalem, which is built as a city: whose houses stand close together within her walls.

4. Thither the tribes go up, even the tribes of the Lord: as it hath been ordained for Israel, to give thanks unto the name of the Lord.

5. For there is set the throne of judgement: even the throne of the house of David.

6. O pray for the peace of Jerusalem: may they prosper that love thee.

7. Peace be within thy walls: and quietness within thy palaces.

8. For my brethren and companions' sakes: I will wish thee prosperity.

9. Because of the house of the Lord our God: I will see to do thee good.

Psalm 123

1. Unto thee lift I up mine eyes: O thou that are enthroned in heaven.
2. Behold, as the eyes of servants look unto the hand of their masters: and as the eyes of a maid unto the hand of her mistress,
3. Even so our eyes look unto the Lord our God: until he shew us his favour.
4. Be gracious unto us O Lord and shew us thy favour: for long have we suffered contempt.
5. Long hath our soul suffered the scorn of the arrogant: and the contempt of them that are proud.

Psalm 124

1. 'If the Lord had not been on our side' now may Israel say: 'if the Lord had not been on our side, when men rose up against us,
2. 'Then they would have swallowed us up alive: when their anger was kindled against us;
3. 'Then the waters would have swept us away, and the torrent gone over us: then the raging waters would have gone clean over us.
4. 'But praised be the Lord: who hath not given us over for a prey unto their teeth.
5. 'We have escaped, as a bird out of the snare of the fowler: the snare is broken, and we are delivered.
6. 'Our help standeth in the name of the Lord: who hath made heaven and earth.'

Psalm 125

1. They that put their trust in the Lord shall be even as the mount Zion: which cannot be moved, but standeth fast for ever.
2. As the hills stand about Jerusalem, so standeth the Lord round about his people: from this time forth for evermore.

3. For the sceptre of wickedness shall not rest upon the land which hath been given to the righteous: lest the righteous put forth their hand to do wickedness.
4. Do good O Lord unto them that are good: and unto them that are upright in heart.
5. As for such as turn aside unto their crooked ways, the Lord shall lead them away with the evildoers: but upon Israel may there be peace.

Psalm 126

1. When the Lord restoreth the fortunes of Zion: then shall we be like unto them that renew their strength.
2. Then shall our mouth be filled with laughter: and our tongue with shouts of joy.
3. Then will they say among the nations: 'The Lord hath done great things for them.'
4. Yea the Lord will do great things for us: whereof we shall be glad.
5. Restore our fortunes O Lord: like as when streams refresh the deserts of the south.
6. They that sow in tears: shall reap with cries of joy.
7. He that goeth forth weeping, and taketh the seed with him: shall come again with gladness, as he bringeth home his sheaves.

Psalm 127

1. Except the Lord build the house: their labour is but lost that build it.
2. Except the Lord keep the city: the watchman waketh but in vain.
3. It is but lost labour that ye rise up early and so late take rest, eating the bread of your toil: for he blesseth his beloved in their beds.
4. Lo, children are an heritage from the Lord: and the fruit of the womb is a gift that cometh from him.

5. Like arrows in the hand of a warrior: even so are the children of a man's youth.
6. Happy is the man that hath his quiver full of them: he shall not be put to shame, when he speaketh with his enemies in the gate.

Psalm 128

1. Blessed are all they that fear the Lord: even they that walk in his ways.
2. Thou shalt eat the labours of thine hands: O well is thee and happy shalt thou be.
3. Thy wife within the walls of thine house: shall be as the fruitful vine;
4. Thy children round about thy table: shall be as the olive branches.
5. Lo thus shall the man be blessed: that feareth the Lord in his heart.
6. May the Lord bless thee out of Zion: mayest thou see Jerusalem in prosperity all thy life long.
7. Mayest thou see thy children's children: and upon Israel may there be peace.

Psalm 129

1. 'Sorely have they afflicted me from my youth up': may Israel now say,
2. 'Sorely have they afflicted me from my youth up . but they have not prevailed against me.
3. 'The ploughers ploughed upon my back: and have made long their furrows.'
4. The Lord is righteous: he hath cut the cords of the ungodly in pieces.
5. Let them be put to shame and turned backward: as many as have evil will for Zion.

6. Let them be even as grass growing upon the house-tops: which withereth before it groweth up,

7. Wherewith the reaper filleth not his hand: neither he that bindeth up the sheaves his bosom;

8. So that they who go by say not 'The blessing of the Lord be upon you: we bless you in the name of the Lord.'

Psalm 130

1. Out of the deep have I called unto thee O Lord: Lord hearken unto my voice.

2. O let thine ears consider well: the voice of my supplications.

3. If thou Lord shouldest mark what is done amiss: O Lord who could abide it?

4. But there is mercy with thee: that so thou mayest be feared.

5. I wait for the Lord, my soul doth wait for him: and in his word is my trust.

6. My soul doth wait for the Lord: more than watchmen for the morning, yea more than watchmen for the morning.

7. Israel trust in the Lord, for with the Lord there is mercy: and with him is plenteous redemption,

8. And he shall redeem Israel: from the multitude of his sins.

Psalm 131

1. O Lord I am not haughty: I have no proud looks.

2. I do not occupy myself with great matters: or with things that are too hard for me.

3. But I have stilled and quieted my soul, as a weaned child upon his mother's breast: so is my soul quieted within me.

4. O Israel trust in the Lord: from this time forth for evermore.

Psalm 132

1. Lord remember David: and all his tribulations;
2. How he sware unto the Lord: and vowed a vow unto the Mighty One of Jacob;
3. 'I will not come within the habitation of my house: nor climb up into my bed;
4. 'I will not suffer mine eyes to sleep: neither shall mine eye-lids slumber,
5. 'Until I find a place for the temple of the Lord: an habitation for the Mighty One of Jacob.'
6. Lo, we heard of the ark of the Lord at Ephrathah: and found it in the fields of Jearim.
7. Let us go into his dwelling-place: and fall low on our knees before his footstool.
8. 'Arise O Lord into thy resting place: thou and the ark of thy strength.
9. 'Let thy priests be clothed with righteousness: and let thy servants sing with joyfulness.
10. 'For thy servant David's sake: reject not thine anointed king.'
11. The Lord hath made a faithful oath unto David: and he will not shrink from it;
12. 'Of the fruit of thy body: shall I set upon thy throne.
13. 'If thy children will keep my covenant, and my testimonies that I shall teach them: their children also shall sit upon thy throne for evermore.'
14. For the Lord hath chosen Zion for himself: he hath desired her for his habitation.
15. 'This shall be my rest for ever: here will I dwell, for I have a delight therein.
16. 'I will bless her victuals with increase: and will satisfy her poor with bread.
17. 'With salvation will I clothe her priests: and her faithful shall rejoice and sing.
18. 'There shall I make the horn of David to flourish: I have prepared a lantern for mine anointed king.

19. 'As for his enemies, I shall clothe them with shame: but upon his head shall his crown be bright.'

Psalm 133

1. Behold how good and lovely a thing it is: when brethren dwell together in unity.
2. It is like the precious ointment upon the head, that ran down unto the beard: even unto Aaron's beard, and flowed down upon his clothing.
3. It is like the dew of Hermon: which falleth upon the hills of Zion.
4. For there the Lord promised his blessing: even life for evermore.

Psalm 134

1. Behold now praise the Lord, all ye servants of the Lord: ye that by night stand in the house of the Lord.
2. Lift up your hands toward the holy place: and sing praises unto the Lord.
3. The Lord that made heaven and earth: give thee blessing out of Zion.

Alternative Psalms

8 God's Glory and Man's Dignity. Praise of Creation.
23 The Lord is my Shepherd. (see p. 27)
25 A prayer for Guidence and protection.
33 A hymn of Praise (The Sea)
46 God is with us.
51 A prayer for forgiveness.
65 Hymn of Praise of God's Creation
84 Longing for God's House (Holy Wells)
91 God our Protector.
93 God the King (Waters of the Sea)
97 Islands and standing stones.
95 An opening psalm for pilgrimages
100 A Hymn of Praise (see p. 46)
139 God's Knowledge and Care.
147 In Praise of God Almighty.
148 All the Earth Praises God.

After each psalm is said Glory be to the Father etc. *and then*

Lord, have mercy upon us.
Christ, have mercy upon us.
Lord, have mercy upon us.

The Our Father, *ending*

v. And lead us not into temptation
r. But deliver us from evil.

The following responses are for use singly or in series:

1 v. I said, Lord, be merciful unto me.
r. Heal my soul, for I have sinned against thee.

2 v. The Lord show thee his ways;
r. And teach thee his paths.

3 v. The Lord direct thy steps according to his word;
r. That no unrighteousness get dominion over thee.

4 v. O that thy ways were made so direct;
r. That thou mightest keep the statutes of the Lord.

5 v. The Lord uphold thy goings in his paths;
r. That thy footsteps slip not.

6 v. Blessed be the Lord God daily;
r. The God of our salvation prosper thy way before thee.

7 v. The good angel of the Lord accompany thee;
r. And dispose thy way and thine actions aright, that thou mayest return again to thine own place with joy.

8 v. Blessed are those that are undefiled in the way;
r. And walk in the law of the Lord.

9 v. Let the enemy have no advantage against thee;
r. And let not the son of wickedness approach to hurt thee.

10 v. O Lord, arise, help us,
r. And deliver us for Thy name's sake.

11 v. Turn us again, O Lord God of hosts;
r. And show the light of thy countenance upon us, and we shall be whole.

12 v. Lord, hear my prayer;
r. And let my crying come unto thee.

13 v. The Lord be with you.
r. And with your spirit.

Concluding Prayers

Let us pray

1 Assist us, O Lord, in these our supplications, and dispose our way towards the attainment of thy salvation, that among all the changes and chances of our journey through life, we may ever be defended by thy help. Through Jesus Christ our Lord. **Amen.**

2 O God, who leadest unto life, and guardest with thy fatherly protection them that trust in thee, we beseech thee that thou wouldest grant unto us an escort of angels; that, being protected by thy aid, we may be shaken by no fear of evil, nor be depressed by any lingering adversity, nor be troubled by any enemy lying in wait to assail us; but that having prosperously accomplished the course of our appointed journey, we may return unto our own homes; and having been received back in safety, may pay due thanks unto thy name. Through Jesus Christ our Lord. **Amen.**

3 O God, who ever bestowest thy pity upon them that love thee, and who are in no placc, far distant from them that serve thee; direct the way of thy servants according to thy will, that thou being their protector and guide, they may walk without stumbling in the paths of righteousness. Through Jesus Christ our Lord. **Amen.**

A Prayer of St. Chrysostom

4 Almighty God, who hast given us grace at this time with one accord to make our common supplications unto thee; and dost promise, that when two or three are gathered together in Thy Name thou wilt grant their requests; fulfil now, O Lord, the desires and petitions of thy servants, as may be most expedient for them; granting us in this world knowledge of thy truth, and in the world to come life everlasting. **Amen.**

5 Into the way of peace and prosperity may the almighty and merciful Lord direct us: and may his Angel Raphael go with us on our journey, that we may return to our homes in peace, safety and joy. **Amen.**

6 O God, who madest the children of Israel to go on dry land through the midst of the sea, and who shewedst to the Magi the way to thyself by the guidance of a star; grant unto thy servants, we beseech thee, a prosperous journey and a quiet time, that, attended by thy holy Angel, we may safely arrive at the place whither we would go, and at length come to the haven of eternal salvation; through Jesus Christ our Lord. **Amen.**

7 O God, who didst bring Abraham thy servant out of Ur of the Chaldees, and preserve him unhurt throughout his journeyings; we beseech thee to take us thy servants under thy protection; be to us, O Lord, a support in setting out, a solace on the way, a shadow in the heat, a covering from the rain and cold, a chariot in weariness, a protection in danger, a staff in slippery places, a harbour in shipwreck, that under thy guidance we may happily reach the place whither we are going, and at length return in safety to our own dwelling; through Jesus Christ our Lord. **Amen.**

8 Grant, we beseech thee, Almighty God, that thy family may walk in the way of salvation, and, by following the counsels of St. John the Forerunner, may come in safety unto him whom he preached, thy Son, Jesus Christ our Lord; who liveth and reigneth with thee in the unity of the Holy Spirit, God world without end. **Amen.**

At the end of the Concluding Prayer the following versicle and response may be said

v. Let us go forth in peace
r. In the name of Christ, Amen.

Please turn to p. 46 for a sequence of prayers for arrival in the City and for the Cathedral Stations.

THE DEWISLAND PILGRIMAGE WALK

The chapels of St. Non with its Holy Well, St. Justinian and St. Patrick are worth a visit. The thirteen-mile round trip from the Cathedral (ten by a shorter route) makes a good day's walk and may be used as a pilgrimage if the chapels and other stopping places on the way are treated as stations for prayer and thought. The constant presence of the sea and of the views of Ramsey Island provoke such pauses. Extracts from the Eastern Orthodox Blessing of the Waters and from Celtic writings are used below to provide six stations. Twelve landmarks are indicated on the map and the reader is invited to use the gradual psalms (p. 10) or the material in the second half of the book to construct the other six stations to his or her own taste.

1 St. Non's Chapel and Holy Well

St. Non's Chapel marks the site of Saint David's birthplace and is dedicated to his mother, St. Non. Tradition has it that the place of his birth shone with so serene a light that it glistened as though the sun was visible and God had brought it in front of the clouds!

In common with many early Christian churches the Chapel may have been built on a Druidical site. The stones of a Bronze Age stone circle can be seen in the field around it. A further tradition is that to relieve the agony of her labour pains Non supported herself on a stone that lay near her and that it retained the prints of her fingers. It is said that when the Chapel was later built on that spot the stone was introduced as an altar table.

Every little chapel had its Holy Well, many taken over from the Druids and christianised, the waters used for Baptism and the needs of the Chapel. St. Non's Holy Well was also a healing well, used for rheumatism and eye maladies. The three steps inside and the stone seat for the Pilgrims are still in place.

> Hast thou heard the saying of Nonn?
> The mother of Saint David was she—
> There is no madness like contention.
>
> *Rhys Goch: The Sayings of the Wise*

Sprinkling at The Holy Well of St. Non

The well spring is a symbol of the basic source of life. The site of the celtic saints' dwelling is marked by a holy well to which the saints were often divinely led and from which they derived natural refreshment. Water is necessary for physical survival, let alone cleanliness, health and comfort; and it is necessary for baptism. The sacramental intermingling of the natural and the supernatural is very much in the Celtic Christian tradition. Water is not brought from somewhere and poured in a font: it is living water, springing forth from the ground. One may go down steps into the well —for, as may be found in many ancient baptisteries, baptism is both a cleansing and going down into the death of Christ, and rising with him in new life. Holy Sprinkling is a natural sacramental action, when, by the use of water as a sign and pledge of God's grace, we are enabled to receive inward and spiritual healing.

Collect

Graciously hear us, God our Saviour, that as we rejoice in the memory of blessed Non we may be instructed in the love of pious devotion. Through Jesus Christ our Lord.

In the name of the Father, and of the Son, and of the Holy Spirit. **Amen.**

v. The Lord be with you.
r. And also with you.

The Priest may briefly introduce the rite. Either:

Let us listen to the Gospel of the Lord.

Jesus said: "Come to me, all you who labour and are overburdened, and I will give you rest. Your heavenly Father knows you have need of all these things".

or (My brothers and sisters). We have come together in the name of our Lord Jesus Christ, who restored the sick to health, and who himself suffered so much for our sake. He is present among us as we recall the words of the apostle James: "Is there anyone sick among you? Let him call for the elders of the Church, and let them pray over him and anoint him in the name of the Lord. This prayer, made in faith, will save the sick man. The Lord will restore his health, and if he had comitted any sins, they will be forgiven."

Let us commend ourselves and each other to the grace and power of Jesus Christ, that the Lord may ease our suffering and grant us health and salvation.

To prepare ourselves for this holy sprinkling, let us call to mind our sins.

Lord Jesus, you healed the sick:

Lord, have mercy.

r. Lord, have mercy.

Lord Jesus, you forgave sinners:

Christ, have mercy.

r. Christ, have mercy.

Lord Jesus, you give us yourself to heal us and bring us strength.

Lord, have mercy.

r. Lord, have mercy.

May almighty God have mercy upon us, forgive us our sins, and bring us to everlasting life. **Amen.**

The Priest might read one of the following passages of scripture—
Matt. 8: 5-10 or 13-17 or Mark 2: 1-12
or the Sprinkling may take place immediately.

Pilgrims normally stand to be sprinkled. They may drink the water, the sign of God's life being given to the soul; the sign of the Cross is made on their forehead in remembrance of their baptism; they may make a cup with their hands and scoop the water in them applying the water to any part of their bodies.

The priest sprinkles assembled pilgrims saying

May Almighty God, at the intercession of Saint David and Saint Non, grant you health and peace.

Psalm 42

As a deer longs for the running brooks: so longs my soul for you, O God.
My soul is thirsty for God, thirsty for the living God: when shall I come and see his face?
My tears have been my food day and night: while they ask me all day long 'Where now is your God?'
As I pour out my soul by myself, I remember this: how I went to the house of the Mighty One, into the temple of God.
To the shouts and song of thanksgiving: a multitude keeping high festival.
Why are you so full of heaviness, my soul: and why so unquiet within me?
O put your trust in God: for I will praise him yet, who is my deliverer and my God.
My soul is heavy within me: therefore I will remember you from the land of Jordan, from Mizar among the hills of Hermon.
Deep calls to deep in the roar of your waters:
all your waves and breakers have gone over me.

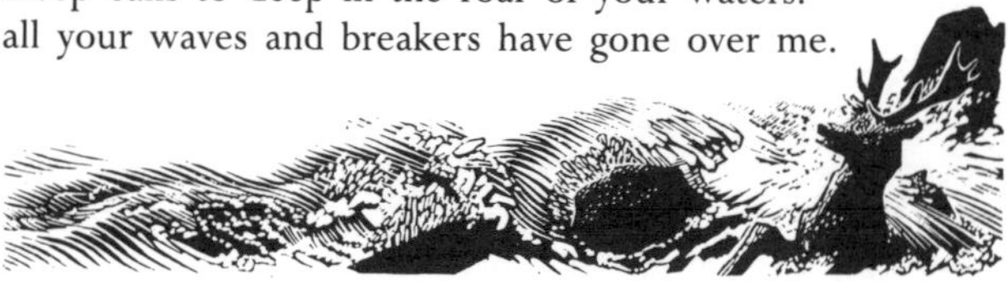

Surely the Lord will grant his loving mercy in the day-time: and in the night his song will be with me, a prayer to the God of my life.
I will say to God, my rock, 'Why have you forgotten me: why must I go like a mourner because the enemy oppresses me?'
Like a sword through my bones, my enemies have mocked me: while they ask me all day long 'Where now is your God?'
Why are you so full of heaviness, my soul: and why so unquiet within me?
O put your trust in God: for I will praise him yet, who is my deliverer and my God.

Glory be to the Father, and to the Son: and to the Holy Spirit;

As it was in the beginning is now, and ever shall be: world without end. **Amen.**

Let us pray
Lord, in your mercy give us living water, always springing up as a fountain of salvation: free us, body and soul, from every danger and admit us to your presence in purity of heart. Grant this through Christ our Lord. **Amen.**

Lord, through this holy sprinkling, come and comfort us with your love and mercy.

Lord, in your mercy . . . r. Hear our prayer.

Free us from all harm.

Lord, in your mercy . . . r. Hear our prayer.

Relieve the sufferings of all the sick here present.

Lord, in your mercy . . . r. Hear our prayer.

Assist all those dedicated to the care of the sick.

Lord, in your mercy . . . r. Hear our prayer.

Free us from sin and all temptation.

Lord, in your mercy . . . r. Hear our prayer.

Give life and health to our brothers and sisters who have been sprinkled in your name.

Lord, in your mercy . . . r. Hear our prayer.

Let us pray for the coming of God's kingdom when sickness and pain shall be no more, in the words that Jesus taught us . . .

Our Father

O Almighty God, who has knit together Thine elect in one communion and fellowship in the mystical Body of Thy Son, Christ our Lord; grant us grace so to follow Thy Blessed Saint Non in all virtuous and godly living, that we may come to those unspeakable joys, which Thou hast prepared for them that unfeignedly love Thee; through Jesus Christ our Lord. **Amen.**

May God the Father bless you, May God the Son heal you,
May God the Holy Spirit enlighten you.
May God protect you from harm and grant you salvation.
May he shine on your heart and lead you to eternal life.
And the blessing of God Almighty, Father, Son and Holy Spirit, come upon you and remain with you for ever. **Amen.**

2 Capel y Pistyll, Porthclais

When David was baptised by Bishop Elvis at Porthclais, near the mouth of the River Alun, a spring burst from the ground at the place to supply the water for his baptism. This spot is marked by a stone well edifice with a v-shaped runnel inserted to pipe the water. Hence the name Capel y Pistyll, the Pipe or Cistern Chapel. There may have been an oratory nearby to mark the sacred place.

v. Perfect Thou my goings in Thy paths that my footsteps be not moved:
r. Incline Thy ear unto me, and hear my words.

Reading Rhygyfarch's 'Life of Saint David'

He (David) was then baptized by Elvis (Ailbe) a bishop of the Munstermen; and he opened they eyes of Movi, who held him under the water, and whose eyes the water splashed, and revealed to him the light of day, which he had never known. In that same place there suddenly appeared a spring for the ministration of baptism.

Psalm 23

The Lord is my shepherd:
therefore can I lack nothing.
He shall make me to lie down in green pastures:
and lead me forth in the right way for his name's sake.
Yea, though I walk through the darkest valley, I will fear no evil:
for thou art with me, thy rod and thy staff comfort me.
Thou shalt prepare a table before me, in the presence of them that trouble me:
thou hast anointed my head with oil, and my cup shall be full.
Yea thy loving kindness and mercy shall follow me all the days of my life:
and I will dwell in the house of the Lord for ever.

Let us pray

We beseech Thee, O Lord, to send Thy grace before us to guide our steps, and sending it with us, be pleased to accompany us on our way; that by the protection of Thy mercy, we may rejoice both in our progress and in our safety. Through Our Lord Jesus Christ. **Amen.**

v. Direct my steps according to Thy word;
and let no iniquity have dominion over me.

r. I rejoiced at the things that were said to me: we shall go into the house of the Lord. Alleluia.

3 The Blessing of the Waters

Christ is baptized and the whole world is made holy; he wipes out the debt of our sins; we will all be purified by water and the Holy Spirit.

Antiphon

Jesus came into our world as Light shining in darkness. 'In him was life, and the life was the light of men. The light shines in the darkness and the darkness has not overcome it.'

Christians have been called to see Jesus Christ everywhere as the Light of God's loving presence. He is the Light of the World and is present through the power of the Incarnation in all created being. He is the Word made flesh. 'For as the rain and the snow come down from heaven, and return not thither but water the earth, making it bring forth and sprout, giving seed to the sower and bread to the eater, so shall my word be that goes forth from my mouth, it shall not return to me empty, but it shall accomplish that which I purpose, and prosper in the thing for which I sent it.' 'For you shall go out in joy; and be let forth in peace; the mountains and hills before you shall break forth into singing, and all the trees of the field shall clap their hands.' The whole created world has been created in God's word (Col. 1:16). Nothing exists or moves to perfection except by God's creative power immanently present in all things.

God pulsates with his silent energies in all of animate nature: grasses, trees, the waters, birds and animals cry out unceasingly to the pilgrim, 'in Him we live and move and have our being.' (Acts. 17:28) The Word is spoken in the mountains, lakes and seas; it goes forth and it does not return empty:

> O Lord, how manifold are thy works!
> In wisdom hast thou made them all;
> The earth is full of thy creatures.
> Yonder is the sea, great and wide,
> Which teems with things innumerable,
> Living things both small and great.
>
> *Ps. 104: 24,25*

Yet the whole of creation is disordered. It is not only mankind who is infected with the nameless woe of a disorientated relationship with the Creator. The whole of Creation shares the same fate of unfulfillment without the Redeemer.

> We know that the whole creation has been groaning in travail together until now; and not only creation, but we ourselves, who have the first fruits of the Spirit, groan inwardly as we wait for adoption as sons, the redemption of our bodies.
> *Rom. 8: 22-23*

Although he was without sin, Jesus Christ came in a body as physical as any sinful body. He became like us in all things save sin, and took upon himself the sin of the whole world.

At his baptism in the Jordan, Jesus received a vision as he came out of the water. He saw the Spirit in the form of a gentle dove and heard his Father declare from on high, 'Thou art my beloved Son; with thee I am well pleased.' It is a moment of ecstatic oneness with the Father, and the baptism at the hands of John is seen as anticipating our own. At the same time it is given a cosmic significance: the sinless Saviour enters the streams of the Jordan, thereby cleansing the waters and imparting grace and redemption to the entire material creation. As he goes up out of the water, he carries the created world up with him. He sees split open the heaven which Adam had closed against himself and his posterity, when he caused the gates of Paradise to be shut with a flaming sword. They are opened, the waters of the sea are made sweet, the earth is glad, the mountains and hills rejoice . . . because Christ is baptised in the Jordan river by John.

As the water falls over his human body, so the love of the Father for him as His Beloved Son cascades over him, covering him with glory; God and matter become one in the Son, the Word, 'because God wanted all perfection to be found in Him and all things to be reconciled through Him and for Him, everything in heaven and everthing on earth.'(Col. 1: 19-20) The world is charged with the grandeur of God.

By the word of the Lord the heavens were made,
and all their host by the breath of his mouth.
He gathered the waters of the sea as in a bottle;
he puts the deeps in storehouses.

Ps. 33:6

Through his Incarnation, made manifest in the symbol of His Baptism, Christ is at the heart of all matter, creating out of love this or that unique creature. He is mystically present in all created nature. His presence may be felt in the breath of the wind and the roar of the sea. Truly, not only 'by the word of the Lord the heavens were made' but the whole created world has been created in Him. We need to affirm that presence, shining forth to us at every moment in our lives.

The Eastern Orthodox rite of the Blessing of the Waters is a beautiful meditation on the relationship between the Lord of all creation and his creature, water. The following office is adapted from the Orthodox service and is an ideal ritual for praising The King of the Sea. As we walk the coastal path to St. Justinian's Chapel, we may remember the Celtic saints, like Justinian himself who lived here, looking out over the sea, listening to the waves breaking on the rocks and to the gulls' cry, seeing the headland of rock jutting out into the sea, the flock of birds, the splendid sunsets—and seeing God in all of it; blessing the Lord who is in all of it and above all things.

Through the waters, the traffic of the seas, ancient links were formed between Eastern Orthodoxy and Celtic spirituality. The archaeology of the area bears witness to them; the prayers perpetuate them.

Readings from The Office of the Blessing of the Waters

The voice of the Lord crieth out over the waters, saying: Come, receive ye all the spirit of wisdom, the spirit of understanding, the spirit of the fear of God, even Christ who is made manifest.
Today is the nature of water sanctified, and Jordan is cloven asunder, and rolleth back the current of its flood, as it beholdeth the Lord baptized.
As a man didst thou come unto that river, O Christ our King, and didst earnestly desire to receive the baptism of a servant, O Good One, at the hands of the Forerunner, because of our sins, O Thou who lovest mankind. Glory to the Father, and to the Son, and to the Holy Spirit, now, and ever, and unto ages of ages. **Amen.**

Unto the voice of him crying in the wilderness: Prepare ye the way of the Lord: thou didst come forth, O Lord, having taken on the form of a servant, and asking baptism, though thou knewest not sin. The waters beheld thee and were affrighted. The Baptist became all trembling, and cried aloud, saying: How shall the candlestick illumine the light? How shall a slave lay hands upon his Lord? Sanctify thou me and these waters, O Saviour, who takest away the sins of the world.

The Parable from the prophesy of Isaiah Isaiah 55: 6-13

Seek the Lord while he may be found,
call upon him while he is near;
let the wicked forsake his way,
and the unrighteous man his thoughts;
let him return to the Lord, that he
may have mercy on him,
and to our God, for he will abundantly pardon.
For my thoughts are not your thoughts,
neither are your ways my ways, says the Lord.
For as the heavens are higher than the earth,
so are my ways higher than your ways
and my thoughts than your thoughts.
For as the rain and the snow come down from heaven,
and return not thither but water the earth,
making it bring forth and sprout,
giving seed to the sower and bread to the eater,
so shall my word be that goes forth from my mouth;
it shall not return to me empty,
but it shall accomplish that which I purpose,
and prosper in the thing for which I sent it.
For you shall go out in joy,
and be led forth in peace;
the mountains and the hills before you
shall break forth into singing
and all the trees of the field shall
clap their hands.
Instead of the thorn shall come up the cypress;
instead of the brier shall come up the myrtle;
and it shall be to the Lord for a memorial,
for an everlasting sign which shall not be cut off.

v. Peace be with you all.
r. And with your spirit.

With joy you will draw water from the wells of salvation.
And you will say in that day:
'Give thanks to the Lord,
call upon his name;
make known his deeds among the nations,
proclaim that his name is exalted.

'Sing praises to the Lord, for he has done gloriously;
let this be known in all the earth.
Shout, and sing for joy, O inhabitant of Zion,
for great in your midst is thy Holy One of Israel.'

Isaiah 12: 3-6

v. The Lord is my light and my salvation, whom shall I fear?
r. The Lord is the strength of my life; of whom shall I be afraid?

Lesson I Cor: 1-4

I want you to know, brethren, that our fathers were all under the cloud, and all passed through the sea, and all baptized into Moses in the cloud and in the sea, and all ate the same supernatural food and all drank the same supernatural drink. For they drank from the supernatural Rock which followed them, and the Rock was Christ.

Verse: The voice of the Lord upon the waters, the God of glory hath thundered: the Lord upon many waters.

v. Peace be with you all.
r. And with your spirit.

Gospel Mark 1: 9-11

In those days Jesus came from Nazareth of Galilee and was baptized by John in the Jordan. And when he came out of the water, immediately he saw the heavens opened and the Spirit descending upon him like a dove; and a voice came from heaven, 'Thou are my beloved Son; with thee I am well pleased'.

Litany

In peace let us pray to the Lord:

For healthful seasons; for abundance of the fruits of the earth; and for peaceful times:

r. Lord have mercy.

For those who travel by sea or land; for the sick and suffering; for those who are in captivity, and for their salvation:
r. Lord have mercy.

That these waters may be sanctified by the power, and effectual operation, and descent of the Holy Spirit:
r. Lord have mercy.

That there may descend upon these waters the cleansing operation of the super-substantial Trinity:
r. Lord have mercy.

That he will endue them with the grace of redemption, the blessing of Jordan, the might, and operation, and descent of the Holy Spirit:
r. Lord have mercy.

That Satan may speedily be crushed under our feet, and that every evil council directed against us may be brought to nought:
r. Lord have mercy.

That the Lord our God will free us from every attack and temptation of the enemy, and make us worthy of the good things which he hath promised:
r. Lord have mercy.

That he will illumine us with the light of understanding and of piety, and with the descent of the Holy Spirit:
r. Lord have mercy.

That this water may be a fountain welling forth unto life eternal:
r. Lord have mercy.

That he will graciously enable us to perfect sanctification by participation in these waters, through the invisible manifestation of the Holy Spirit:
r. Lord have mercy.

That the Lord will hearken unto the voice of petition of us sinners, and will have mercy upon us:

r. Lord have mercy.

That he will deliver us from all tribulation, wrath, and necessity:

r. Lord have mercy.

Succour us, save us, have mercy upon us, and keep us, O God, by thy grace.

r. Lord have mercy.

Let us pray.

O Lord Jesus Christ, the Only-begotten Son, who art in the bosom of the Father, the true God, Source of Life and of Immortality; Light of Light, who art come into the world to illuminate it: enlighten our minds with thy Holy Spirit, and accept us who offer unto thee majesty and thanksgiving for thy marvellous mighty works, which are from all eternity; as, also, for thy saving providence in these latter ages, in which thou hast clothed thyself in our frail and lowly substance, and hast condescended to the stature of a servant; who yet art King of all; who also didst receive baptism in Jordan at the hands of a servant: that thou, O Sinless One, having sanctified the nature of water, mightest make for us a way which should be unto a new birth, through water and the Spirit, and unto the deliverance then first instituted for us. Celebrating the memory of which divine majesty, we beseech thee, O Lord who lovest mankind, sprinkle us, thine unworthy servants, according to thy divine promise, with pure water, the gift of thy tenderness of heart. And may the supplications of us sinners over this holy water be well pleasing unto thy goodness: and may thy blessing through it be vouchsafed unto us, and unto all thy faithful people, to the glory of thy holy and adorable Name.
For unto thee belongeth all glory, honour and worship, together with thy Father who is from everlasting, and thine all-holy, and good, and life-giving Spirit, now, and ever, and unto ages of ages. **Amen.**

Great art thou, O Lord, and marvellous are thy works, and speech sufficeth not to sing the praises of thy wonders. For thou, by thy will, from nothingness hast brought all things into being; by thy majesty thou dost uphold all creation, and by thy providence thou dost direct the world. When thou hadst framed the universe out of four elements, thou didst crown the circle of the year with four seasons. All the reason-endowed powers tremble before thee. The Sun singeth thy praises, and the Moon glorifieth thee; the Stars, also, stand before thy presence. The Light obeyeth thee. The deeps shudder with awe before thee; the water-springs do thy bidding. Thou hast spread out the heavens like a curtain. Thou hast established the earth upon the waters. With sand hast thou walled in the sea. Thou hast shed abroad the air for breathing. The Angelic Powers serve thee. The Archangelic hosts adore thee. The many-eyed Cherubim and the six-winged Seraphim, as they stand round about and do fly, veil their faces with awe before thine unapproachable glory. For thou, the God which cannot be circumscribed, who art from everlasting and ineffable, didst come down upon earth, taking on the form of a servant, and being made in the likeness of men. For thou couldst not endure, O Master, because of thy tender-hearted mercy, to behold the children of men tormented by the devil; but thou didst come, and didst save us. We confess thy grace; we proclaim thy mercy; we conceal not thy gracious deeds. Thou hast set at liberty the generations of our race; by thy birth thou hast sanctified a Virgin's womb. All creation singeth praises unto thee, who didst reveal thyself; for thou, our God, didst manifest thyself upon earth, and didst dwell among men. Thou didst hallow, also, the streams of Jordan, in that thou didst send down from heaven thy Holy Spirit, and didst crush the heads of the serpents which lurked there. Wherefore do thou, O King, who lovest mankind, come down now also through the descent of thy Holy Spirit, and sanctify this water. And impart unto it the grace of redemption, the blessing of Jordan.

Make it a fountain of immortality, a gift of sanctification, a remission of sins, a healing of infirmities, a destruction of demons; unapproachable by hostile powers, filled with angelic might. And may it be unto all those who shall draw it, and shall partake of it unto the purification of their souls and bodies, unto the healing of their passions, unto the sanctification of their houses, and unto every expedient service. For thou art our God, who through water and the Spirit does renew our nature, which had fallen into decay through sin. For thou art our God, who with water didst drown sin in the days of Noah. For thou art our God, who by the sea, through Moses, didst set free from slavery to Pharaoh the Hebrew race. For thou art our God, who didst cleave the rock in the wilderness so that water gushed forth, and who madest the floods to well forth abundantly; and didst satisfy thy thirsty people. For thou art our God, who by fire and water, through Elijah, didst set Israel free from the errors of Baal.

Do thou, the same Master, sanctify now also this water by thy Holy Spirit.

Grant also unto all who shall be sprinkled therewith, and shall partake thereof, and shall anoint themselves therewith, sanctification, blessing, purification and bodily health.

Incline thine ear, O Lord, and hear us, O thou who was graciously pleased to receive baptism in Jordan, and didst sanctify the waters. Bless all us who, by the bowing of our necks, do outwardly signify our humility of mind: and graciously grant that we may be filled with thy sanctification, through our partaking of this water, and through sprinkling therewith. And may be it unto us, O Lord, for the health of our souls and bodies.

For thou art the sanctification of our souls and bodies, and unto thee we ascribe glory, and thanksgiving and worship, together with thy Father, who is from everlasting, and thine all-holy, and good, and life giving Spirit, now, and ever, and unto ages of ages. **Amen.**

When in Jordan thou wast baptized, O Lord, the worship of the Trinity was made manifest. For the voice of the Father bore witness unto thee, calling thee his beloved Son, and the Spirit, in the form of a dove, confirmed the steadfastness of that word. O Christ, who didst manifest thyself, and dost enlighten the world, glory to thee.

May he who was graciously pleased to accept baptism from John, in Jordan, for the sake of our salvation, Christ our true God, through the prayers of his most pure Mother, and of all the Saints, have mercy upon us and save us: forasmuch as he is gracious and loveth mankind. **Amen.**

4. Ramsey Island (viewed on the path to St. Justinian)

Delightful I think it to be in the bosom of an isle, on the peak of a rock, that I might often see there the calm of the sea.

That I might see its heavy waves over the glittering ocean, as they chant a melody to their Father on their eternal course.

That I might see its smooth strand of clear headlands, no gloomy thing; that I might hear the voice of the wondrous birds, a joyful tune.

That I might hear the sound of the shallow waves against the rocks; that I might hear the cry by the graveyard, the noise of the sea.

That I might see its splendid flocks of birds over the full-watered ocean; that I might see its mighty whales, greatest of wonders.

That I might see its ebb and its flood-tide in their flow; that this might be my name, a secret I tell, 'He who turned his back on Ireland.'

That contrition of heart should come upon me as I watch it; that I might bewail my many sins, difficult to declare.

That I might bless the Lord who has power over all, Heaven with its pure host of angels, earth, ebb, flood-tide.

That I might pore on one of my books, good for my soul; a while kneeling for beloved Heaven, a while at psalms.

A while gathering dulse from the rock, a while fishing, a while giving food to the poor, a while in my cell.

A while meditating upon the Kingdom of Heaven, holy is the redemption; a while at labour not too heavy; it would be delightful!

St. Columba's Island Heritage

Irish; author unknown; 12th Century

Celtic Prayer

May God
open to me
every pass.

Christ
open to me
every narrow way.

Each soul of
holy man and woman
in heaven

Be preparing for me
my pathway.

5 St. Justinian's Chapel

The ruins overlooking Ramsey Sound are those of a Chapel built by Bishop Vaughan in the sixteenth century on the site of an older building possibly a celtic oratory. St. Justinian was a hermit, born in Brittany, and a friend of Saint David. He was murdered on Ramsey Island, walked across the Sound with his head in his arms and laid himself to rest on the spot marked by his Chapel. His remains were later taken into the Cathedral where they are reputed to have been interred with the relics of Saint David.

The Beatitudes Luke 6: 20-38

Blessed are you poor, for yours is the kingdom of God.
Blessed are you that hunger now, for you shall be satisfied.
Blessed are you that weep now, for you shall laugh.
Blessed are you when men hate you, and when they exclude and revile you, and cast out your name as evil, on account of the Son of man!
Rejoice in that day, and leap for joy, for behold, your reward is great in heaven; for so their fathers did to the prophets.
But woe to you that are rich, for you have received your consolation.
Woe to you that laugh now, for you shall mourn and weep.
Woe to you, when all men speak well of you, for so their fathers did to the false prophets.
But I say to you that hear, love your enemies, do good to those who hate you, bless those who curse you, pray for those who abuse you.
To him who strikes you on the cheek, offer the other also; and from him who takes away your coat do not withhold even your shirt. Give to every one who begs from you; and of him who takes away your goods do not ask them again.
And as you wish that men would do to you, do so to them.
If you love those who love you, what credit is that to you? For even sinners love those who love them.
And if you do good to those who do good to you, what credit is that to you? For even sinners do the same. And if you lend to those from whom you hope to receive, what credit is that to you? Even sinners lend to sinners, to receive as much again.

But love your enemies, and do good, and lend, expecting nothing in return; and your reward will be great, and you will be sons of the Most High; for he is kind to the ungrateful and the selfish.
Be merciful, and as your Father is merciful.
Judge not, and you will not be judged; condemn not, and you will not be condemned; forgive, and you will be forgiven; give, and it will be given to you; good measure, pressed down, shaken together, running over, will be put into your lap. For the measure you give will be the measure you get back.

Praise God for His mercies to you on this Pilgrimage.
Praise Him for all His Saints, and especially for the Life and Witness of St. Justinian.
Pray for God's Blessing on all those who have taken part in the Pilgrimage.
Pray that in the years to come, there may be many Pilgrimages made to the Shrine of St. David.

v. They shall go from strength to strength.
r. And unto the God of Gods appeareth every one of them in Zion.

Let us pray
O Almighty God, Who in all ages has led Thy servants to seek the Light: Grant to us Thy Heavenly guidance and merciful protection, and that when our Pilgrimage on earth is ended we may rest for ever in Thy Heavenly country. Through Jesus Christ our Lord. **Amen.**

Lead us, O Lord, in all our doings with thy most gracious favour, and further us with thy continual help; that in all our works begun, continued, and ended in thee, we may glorify thy holy name, and finally by thy mercy obtain everlasting life. Through Jesus Christ our Lord. **Amen.**

Collect

May the intercession of the blessed Justinian help us, we pray You, Lord, so that we may obtain by his patronage what we cannot receive by our own merits. Through Jesus Christ our Lord.

Thoughts From the Gaelic

God's will would I do:
My own will bridle;

God's due would I give:
My own due yield;

God's path would I travel:
My own path refuse;

Christ's death would I ponder:
My own death remember;

Christ's agony would I meditate:
My love to God make warmer;

Christ's cross would I carry:
My own cross forget;

Repentance of sin would I make:
Early repentance choose;

A bridle to my tongue would I put:
A bridle on my thoughts I would keep;

God's judgement would I judge:
My own judgement guard;

Christ's redemption would I seize:
My own ransom work;

The love of Christ would I feel:
My own love know.

6 St. Patrick's Chapel

Legend says the chapel marked the site of St. Patrick's home, from which he was stolen by pirates and taken to Ireland. It has also been suggested that it marks the spot in Porth Mawr from which he later sailed to unify the Irish church; there is also the 'Seat', Eisteddfa Badrig, from which the mountains of Ireland are visible. Whatever the occasion, it most certainly was a holy station for early pilgrims on their way to and from Ireland and the settlement of St. David's. Ireland returned the compliment later, for there are churches dedicated to Saint David in the Irish dioceses of Cloyne, Ferns and Kildare.

Reading Rhygyfarch's Life of St. David

Patrick, polished with Roman learning, came to the country of the people of Ceredigion wherein he sojourned a little while. He entered the country of Dyfed and there wandering about arrived at length at the place which was named Vallis Rosina; and perceiving that the place was pleasant, he vowed to serve God faithfully there. But when he was revolving these things in his mind an Angel of the Lord appeared to him: 'God,' said he, 'hath not disposed this place for thee, but for a son who is not yet born, nor will be until thirty years are past.' Patrick remonstrated with the angel who, because the Lord loved Patrick much, coaxed him with kindly words, saying, 'Rejoice, Patrick, for the Lord hath sent me to thee that I may show thee the whole of the island of Ireland from the seat which is in Vallis Rosina. Exult, Patrick, for thou shalt be the Apostle of the whole of that island which thou seest.' At these words he raised his eyes and beheld the whole island.
At length he cheerfully quitted the sacred spot for holy David, and preparing a ship in Porth Mawr he sailed for Ireland.

Thank God for the life and witness of St. Patrick.
Praise God for His Glory revealed in his blessed saints.
Pray that there may never be wanting sons and daughters of

the Celtic Churches, who shall carry forth the glorious message of the Gospel.

Pray for the Church in Wales.

Pray that God may bless all her missionary undertakings.

v. Their sound has gone out into all lands.
r. And their words unto the ends of the world.

Let us pray

O God, who through the ministry of thy servant Patrick, didst proclaim the message of Thy Holy Gospel, grant, we beseech thee, that following the example of his constancy and zeal, we may come to the light of everlasting life; through Jesus Christ our Lord. **Amen.**

O Lord Jesus Christ, who hast said to thine Apostles 'Peace I leave with you, my peace I give unto you,' regard not our sins, but the faith of thy Church, and grant unto her that peace and unity which are acceptable to Thy Will; who livest and reignest with the Father and the Holy Spirit, One God, for ever and ever. **Amen.**

Saint Patrick's Breastplate

I bind unto myself today
The strong name of the Trinity:
By invocation of the same,
The Three in One and One in Three.

I bind this day to me for ever,
By power of faith, Christ's incarnation,
His baptism in the Jordan River,
His death on the Cross for my salvation.
His bursting from the spiced tomb,
His riding up the heavenly way,
His coming at the day of doom
I bind unto myself today!

I bind unto myself today
The power of God to hold and lead:
His eye to watch, his might to stay,
His ear to hearken to my need;
The wisdom of my God to teach,
His hand to guide, his shield to ward;
The Word of God to give me speech,
His heavenly host to be my guard!

Christ be with me, Christ within me,
Christ behind me, Christ before me,
Christ beside me, Christ to win me,
Christ to comfort and restore me.
Christ beneath me, Christ above me,
Christ in quiet, Christ in danger,
Christ in hearts of all that love me,
Christ in mouth of friend and stranger.

I bind unto myself the name,
The strong name of the Trinity:
By invocation of the same,
The Three in One and One in Three;
Of whom all nature hath creation,
Eternal Father, Spirit, Word;
Praise to the Lord of my salvation—
Salvation is of Christ the Lord!

Collect

O God who didst foretell thy blessed confessor and bishop, David, by the message of an angel to Patrick, prophesying thirty years before his birth: we beseech thee that by his intercession, whose memory we are keeping, we may attain to eternal joys. Through Jesus Christ our Lord.

ARRIVAL

At the entrance to the City, the Litany may be chanted or said, or suitable Hymns sung. When the cathedral comes into view, a Station may be made, and Silent Prayer offered.

At the South Porch of the Cathedral

The Pilgrims approach the Cathedral and on reaching the porch, a Station may be made, and the following prayers said:

v. I was glad when they said unto me:
r. We will go into the House of the Lord.

Psalm 100 The Jubilate

1. O be joyful in the Lord all ye lands: serve the Lord with gladness, and come before his presence with a song.
2. Be ye sure that the Lord he is God: it is he that hath made us and we are his; we are his people and the sheep of his pasture.
3. O go your way into his gates with thanksgiving, and into his courts with praise: be thankful unto him and bless his holy name.
4. For the Lord is gracious, his mercy is everlasting: and his faithfulness endureth from generation to generation.

Let us pray

O Almighty God, who didst inspire Thy Holy Servant, David, to preach the Gospel in this land, fill us with Thy Holy Spirit that this Pilgrimage may be to Thy honour and glory, and that we may labour in prayer for the greater Glory of Thy Holy Name. Through Jesus Christ our Lord. **Amen.**

Though we have arrived at the City and at the Cathedral, 'here is no abiding city, here is no continuing stay.' The Christian's whole life on earth is a pilgrimage to God. The Christian Church is on pilgrimage, following in the steps of Abraham, who left his own home and went in faith to an unknown country; following too the Israelites who went through deserts to the Promised Land. Pilgrimage should be seen in that light.

You are asked to remember that this Cathedral of St. Davids was originally founded by the patron Saint of Wales: and you are asked to pray for the divine blessing on it, that it may be increasingly a centre of true faith, conversions, and of healing of souls and bodies.

The Cathedral Prayer

O God, who dwellest not in temples made with hands, and yet dost deign to work in them and by them, pour down thy blessing upon this Cathedral Church of Saint David, and on all who minister herein; grant that it may be in very deed the Mother-Church of the Diocese, a strength and support to thy servant N. our Bishop, a joy and inspiration to the faithful, and a home of prayer and devotion, setting forth to thy people everywhere a pattern of holy and reverent worship. Hear us, O merciful Father, for the sake of thy Son, Jesus Christ our Lord. **Amen.**

A FORM OF RECEPTION FOR PILGRIMS

Greeting Rom. 1: 7

Grace to you and peace from God our Father and the Lord Jesus Christ.

A few personal words of welcome may be given

We welcome you in the name of the Lord who said 'I was a stranger and you welcomed me' and we give thanks unto him for your safe arrival.

Let us pray together that we may be united in peace; hear his holy word; and receive his mercy in the midst of his holy temple.

Let us pray

O God, who didst lead the children of Israel through the Red Sea as upon the dry land, who didst also lead the wise men from the East to the cradle of thy dear Son through the guiding of a star; we thank thee that thou hast granted unto us a prosperous journey, a quiet time, and seasonable weather, and beseech thee that, guided by thine holy angels, we may arrive safely, this life's journey ended, in the land of everlasting life; through Jesus Christ our Lord. **Amen.**

Hear the Holy Gospel according to St. Matthew *(Matt. 25: 31-45)*

When the Son of man comes in his glory, and all the angels with him, then he will sit on his glorious throne. Before him will be gathered all the nations, and he will separate them one from another as a shepherd separates the sheep from the goats, and he will place the sheep at his right hand, but the goats at the left. Then the King will say to those at his right hand, 'Come, O blessed of my Father, inherit the kingdom prepared for you from the foundation of the world; for I was hungry and you gave me food, I was thirsty and you gave me drink, I was a stranger and you welcomed me, I was naked and you clothed me, I was sick and you visited me, I was in prison and you came to me.' Then the righteous will answer him, 'Lord, when did we see thee hungry and feed thee, or thirsty and give thee drink? And when did we see thee a stranger and welcome thee, or naked and clothe thee? And when did we see thee sick or in prison and visit thee?' And the King will answer them, 'Truly, I say to you, as you did it to one of the least of these my brethren, you did it to me.' Then he will say to those at his left hand, 'Depart from me, you cursed, into the eternal fire prepared for the devil and his angels; for I was hungry and you gave me no food, I was thirsty and you gave me no drink, I was a stranger and you did not welcome me, naked and you did not clothe me, sick and in prison and you did not visit me.' Then they also will answer, 'Lord, when did we see thee hungry or thirsty or a stranger or naked or sick or in prison, and did not minister to thee?' Then he will answer them,

'Truly, I say to you, as you did it not to one of the least of these, you did it not to me.'

v. Lord, I have loved the habitation of thy house;

r. And the place where thine honour dwelleth.

A General Thanksgiving **(said by all)**

Almighty God, Father of all mercies,
we thine unworthy servants do give thee most humble and hearty thanks
for all thy goodness and loving-kindness to us and to all men;
we bless thee for our creation, preservation, and all the blessings of this life;
but above all, for thine inestimable love in the redemption of the world by our Lord Jesus Christ, for the means of grace,
and for the hope of glory.
And we beseech thee, give us that due sense of all thy mercies,
that our hearts may be unfeignedly thankful,
and that we show forth thy praise
not only with our lips, but in our lives;
by giving up ourselves to thy service,
and by walking before thee in holiness and righteousness all our days;
through Jesus Christ our Lord,
to whom with thee and the Holy Spirit be all honour and glory,
world without end. **Amen.**

For the Saints

Almighty and everliving God, we praise thy Name for thy servants who have finished their course in thy faith and fear, the blessed Virgin Mary, and holy Patriarchs, Prophets, Apostles, and Martyrs, and all thy righteous servants; and we beseech thee that, encouraged by their example, and strengthened by their fellowship, we also may be partakers of their inheritance in glory; through Jesus Christ our Lord, to whom with thee and the Holy Spirit be all honour and glory, now and for ever. **Amen.**

Let us pray

Lead us, Lord, with thy most gracious favour, and further us with thy continual help; that in all our works, begun, continued, and ended in thee, we may glorify thy holy Name, and finally by thy mercy obtain everlasting life; through Jesus Christ our Lord. **Amen.**

Rhagflaena ni, O Arglwydd, a'th ragorol ras, a hyrwydda ni a'th barhaus gymorth, fel, yn ein holl weithredoedd o'u dechrau i'w diwedd ynot ti y gogoneddwn dy Enw sanctaidd, a chael yn y diwedd gan dy drugaredd fywyd tragwyddol; trwy Iesu Grist ein Harglwydd. **Amen.**

THE CATHEDRAL STATIONS

1. At the Font—A Thanksgiving for Holy Baptism

Reading Romans 6: 3-11

Do you not know that all of us who have been baptized into Christ Jesus were baptized into his death? We were buried therefore with him by baptism into death, so that as Christ was raised from the dead by the glory of the Father, we too might walk in newness of life. For if we have been united with him in a death like his, we shall certainly be united with him in a resurrection like his. We know that our old self was crucified with him so that the sinful body might be destroyed, and we might no longer be enslaved to sin. For he who has died is freed from sin. But if we have died with Christ, we believe that we shall also live with him. For we know that Christ being raised from the dead will never die again; death no longer has dominion over him. The death he died he died to sin, once for all, but the life he lives to God. So you also must consider yourselves dead to sin and alive to God in Christ Jesus.

Think of your own Baptism. Think of all those that have been baptised into the flock of Christ's Church.

Pray that we may never be ashamed to confess the faith of Christ crucified.

Pray that we may have power and strength to have victory and to triumph against the devil, the world and the flesh.

Pray that we may receive the fulness of God's grace, and ever remain in the number of his faithful and elect children.

Let us renew the promises we made in baptism when we rejected Satan and his works, and promised to serve God faithfully in his holy Church.

The Blessing of the water in the Font

We give thanks to thee, O Lord, Holy Father, Almighty, Everlasting God, because thou hast appointed the Water of Baptism for the regeneration of mankind through thy beloved Son; who at his baptism in the river Jordan was anointed with the Holy Spirit; and after his saving Death and mighty Resurrection commanded his Apostles to go and make disciples of all nations, baptizing them in the Name of the Father and of the Son and of the Holy Spirit;

Hear therefore, the prayers of thy Church; sanctify this Water for the mystical washing away of sin, and grant these persons, in the renewing of their Baptismal Promises, may receive the fulness of thy grace, and ever remain among thy faithful and elect children;

Through Christ our Lord, to whom with thee in the unity of the Holy Spirit, be all honour and glory, world without end. **Amen.**

The Promises

v. Do you renounce the works of the devil, the vain glory of the world, and all sinful desires?

r. I renounce them all.

v. Do you believe and trust in God the Father, who made you and all the world; and in his son Jesus Christ, who redeemed you and all mankind; and in the Holy Spirit, who sanctifies you and all the elect people of God?

r. I do so believe and trust.
v. Will you obediently keep God's holy will and commandments all the days of your life?
r. I will, the Lord being my helper.
v. Let us humbly confess our sins to Almighty God.

Almighty God, Father of our Lord Jesus Christ,
We acknowledge and confess that we have sinned in thought, word and deed,
against thy Divine Majesty.
We earnestly repent,
and are heartily sorry for these our misdoings;
Have mercy upon us, most merciful Father;
Forgive us all that is past;
And grant that we may ever hereafter
serve and please thee in newness of life,
To the honour and glory of thy Name;
Through Jesus Christ our Lord. **Amen.**

v. Almighty God have mercy upon you/us; pardon and deliver you/us from all your/our sins, confirm and strengthen you/us in all goodness; and bring you/us to everlasting life; through Jesus Christ our Lord. **Amen.**

The Blessing of pilgrims with blessed water from the font

Let us pray

God, the all-powerful Father of our Lord Jesus Christ, has given us new birth by water and the Holy Spirit, and forgiven all our sins. May He also keep us faithful to our Lord Jesus Christ for ever and ever. **Amen.**

or Grant, O Lord, that as we are baptised into the death of Thy blessed Son, our Saviour, Jesus Christ, so by continued dying to selfishness we may be buried with Him: and that through the grave and gate of death we may pass to our joyful resurrection: for His merits, who died and was buried, and rose again for us, Thy Son, Jesus Christ our Lord. **Amen.**

2. At the People's Altar in the Nave

Let us pray for courage to confess the faith of Christ crucified.

Let us pray that all our countrymen may be drawn to the Cross of Christ.

Let us pray for the spirit of self sacrifice.

Let us pray that we may with all the saints enter into the length and breadth and height of the Cross of Christ.

v. O Saviour of the world, who by thy Cross and precious Blood has redeemed us:

r. Save us and help us, we humbly beseech thee, O Lord.

Almighty God, we beseech thee graciously to behold this thy family, for which our Lord Jesus Christ was content to be betrayed, and given up into the hands of wicked men, and to suffer death upon the Cross, who now liveth and reigneth with thee and the Holy Ghost, ever one God, world without end. **Amen.**

v. We pray thee help thy servants:

r. Whom thou has redeemed with thy precious blood.

O Lord, the Maker and Redeemer of all believers, grant to the faithful departed all the unsearchable benefits of thy Son's passion, that in the day of his appearing they may be manifested as thy children. Through Jesus Christ our Lord. **Amen.**

3. Before the Cross

Adore the lifted standard of the Cross,
O faithful soul.
Who takes it for his sign, need fear no sorrow.
That blessed cross, where the Lord's body hung,
And by his dying, closed the road to death.
He that created life, slew death by dying,
And by his wounds are the world's wounds made whole.

Here, dying for the world, the world's life hung,
Leaving a world's sin in that deathly tide:
That downbent head raised earth upon the stars.
O timeless wonder! Life, because One died.

Alcuin

4. In the Choir

Lord God Almighty, whose glory cherubim and seraphim and all the hosts of heaven with ceasless voice proclaim, hear and accept, we humbly beseech thee, the praises of thy Church below; and pour down upon thy ministers in Choir and Sanctuary such as a spirit of faith, reverence, and joy, as shall lift both their hymns and their lives unto thee, through Jesus Christ our Lord. **Amen.**

May David whose memory we devoutly celebrate on earth, unite us by his intercessions to the angelic choir, God and our Lord Jesus Christ granting it, to whom is honour and glory throughout endless ages of ages. **Amen.**

Adapted from Rhygyfarch: Life of Saint David; concluding words of Section LXV

5. At the Shrine of Saint David

The Shrine of Saint David stands on the North Side of the High Altar and the feretory containing the important relics of Saint David is housed in the Trinity Chapel.

Prayer

O God, Who by the teaching of Thy Blessed Servant, Saint David, didst cause the light of the Gospel to shine in the land of Wales; grant, we beseech Thee, that having his life and his labours in remembrance, we may show forth our thankfulness unto Thee for the same, by following the example of his most holy life, through Jesus Christ our Lord. **Amen.**

David, Christ's glorious bishop, receive the desires of thy servants and intercede for us to our great Lord.
O God, who hast given to thy church blessed David thy bishop for a wonderful teacher: mercifully grant that we may deserve ever to have before thee this loving intercessor. Through . . .

Respond and Collect from the Life of Saint David,
by Giraldus Cambrensis, c. 1146-1223

6. At the High Altar

We sinners beseech thee to hear us, O Lord God, and that it may please thee to rule and govern thy holy Church Universal in the right way;

r. We beseech thee to hear us, good Lord.

That it may please thee to enlighten all Bishops, Priests, and Deacons, with true knowledge and understanding of thy Word, and that both by their preaching and living they may set it forth and show it accordingly;

r. We beseech thee to hear us, good Lord.

That it may please thee to give to all thy people increase of grace to hear gladly thy holy word, and to receive it with pure affection, and to bring forth the fruits of the Spirit;

r. We beseech thee to hear us, good Lord.

Let us pray

O Lord Jesus Christ, who didst charge thine apostles to preach the gospel to every creature: propser, we pray thee, the work of thy Church in this land. Give vision and courage to our bishops and all who exercise spiritual leadership; and so inflame the hearts of thy people with burning love that they may be moved to share with others the blessing of thy redeeming love; who livest and reignest with the Father and the Holy Spirit, one God, for ever and ever. **Amen**

Collect Bangor prayer for Saint David's Day

O God who of thy great love to the Church of the Welsh people didst exalt thy servant Saint David that he might safeguard the faith of the Catholic Church: grant to us, his spiritual children, so to maintain the Faith in its purity, and to serve our country in faithfulness, that with him we may receive the same heavenly reward. Through Jesus Christ . . .

7. In the Chapel of the Most Holy Trinity

Contemplate the Mystery of the Holy and Glorious Trinity.
Contemplate the dazzling Holiness of God.
Contemplate God's unending years.
Contemplate God's call to you, His love for you, the Reward He has in store for you.
Pray that you may evermore serve Him faithfully.
Pray that you may ever help forward His Church in Wales.
Pray that you may live and die constant in your faith.

v. O Holy, Blessed, and Glorious Trinity, three Persons and One God:
r. Have mercy upon us, miserable sinners.

Let us pray

Almighty and everlasting God, Who hast given unto us Thy servants grace by the confession of a true faith to acknowledge the glory of the Eternal Trinity, and in the power of the Divine Majesty to worship the Unity: we beseech Thee that Thou wouldst keep us steadfast in this faith, and evermore defend us from all adversities: Who livest and reignest, One God, world without end. **Amen.**

Prayer Before the Relics of Saint David

Almighty Father
you lead us to heaven
where the door has been opened for us
by Jesus Christ, your Son, our Lord.

We bless you
for that innumerable company gone before us
who showed us the way.

We bless you for DAVID
patron of this country and this cathedral church.

For our safe arrival in this holy place
and for all the blessing of this life
we give you thanks, good Lord.

Bless us here, we pray,
and bring us again to our homes in peace.

Come with us strangers and pilgrims
on our journey through this world
and bring us at last, good Lord,
to our home in heaven;

through Jesus Christ our Lord
who lives and reigns with you and the Holy Spirit
one God for ever and ever. **Amen**

Reading The death of Saint David from *The Book of the Anchorite of Llanddewibrefi* (1346) translated from the Welsh by D. M. Lloyd

And after he had bestowed his blessing on all, he (Saint David) spoke these words: 'Noble brothers and sisters, be glad, and guard your faith and religion and do the little things which you have heard from me, and which I have shown you. And fare you well,' said David, 'and may you conduct be steadfast on the earth. For we shall never meet here again.' And then was heard a cry arising from all, a wail and lamentation and weeping, and people exclaiming 'Woe to us that the earth does not swallow us, that fire does not burn us, would that God would raise the sea over the land, and cause the mountains to fall on us,' and almost all that were present were near unto death. From the Sunday to the Wednesday after David's death they took no meat or drink, but prayed piteously. And Tuesday night, close on cock-crow, lo, a host of angels filled the city, and all places in the city were filled with song and joy. And in the morning hour, behold, Jesus Christ came, accompanied by nine orders of heavenly beings, as when He is surrounded by them in Majesty. And the brilliant sun shone over the whole host. And that Tuesday the first day of March, Jesus Christ bore away David's soul in great triumph and gladness and honour. After his hunger, his thirst, and cold, and his labours, his abstinence and his acts of charity, and his weariness, and his tribulation, and his afflictions, and his anxiety for the world, the angels received his soul, and they bore it to a place where the light does not fail, and there is rest without labour, and joy without sadness, an abundance of all good things, and victory, and brilliance, and beauty; where Christ's champions are commended, and the undeserving rich are ignored, where there is health without sickness, youth without old age, peace without dissension, glory without vain ostentation, songs that do not pall, and rewards without end.

Collect

Almighty and everlasting God who by thy holy angel didst wondrously provide a dwelling place for blessed David thy confessor and bishop ere he was born: mercifully grant unto us that with him, whose merits we venerate upon earth, we may ever enjoy the vision of thee in heaven. Through our Lord . . .

from the Mass of Saint David,
15th Cent. MS, Sarum Missal

Invocation

Bless us, O God, Father, Son and Holy Spirit, with the vision of thy glory; that we may know thee as the Father who created us, rejoice in thee as the Son who redeemed us, and be strong in thee, the Holy Spirit who dost sanctify us; keep us steadfast in this faith, and bring us at the last into thine eternal kingdom where thou art ever worshipped and glorified, one God, world without end.

Nunc Dimittis Luke 2: 29

Lord, now lettest thou thy servant depart in peace:
according to thy word.
For mine eyes have seen thy salvation: which thou hast
prepared before the face of all peoples.

To be a light to lighten the Gentiles: and to be the glory of thy people Israel.
Glory be to the Father, and to the Son: and to the Holy Spirit;
As it was in the beginning, is now, and ever shall be: world without end. **Amen.**

Blessing

May the infinite and glorious Trinity, the Father, the Son and the Holy Spirit, direct our life in good works, and after our journey through this world grant us eternal rest with the saints.

Mozarbic Sacramentary.

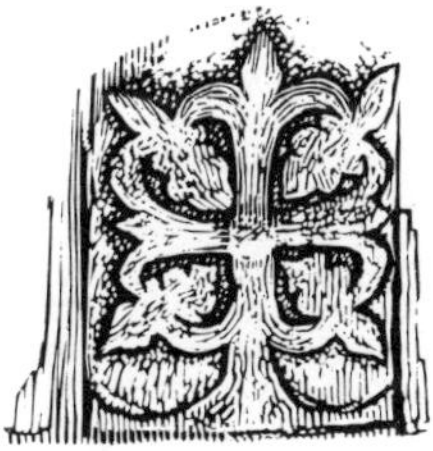

8. In The Chapel of St. Edward—For the Faithful Departed

Psalm 130

Out of the depths have I called to you, O Lord:
Lord, hear my voice.
O let your ears consider well:
the voice of my supplication.
If you, Lord, should note what we do wrong:
who then, O Lord, could stand?
But there is forgiveness with you:
so that you shall be feared.
I wait for the Lord, my soul waits for him:
and in his word is my hope.
My soul looks for the Lord:
more than watchmen for the morning,
more, I say, than watchmen for the morning.

O Israel, trust in the Lord,
for with the Lord there is mercy:
and with him is ample redemption.
He will redeem Israel:
from the multitude of his sins.

Pray that the Church in Wales may ever maintain the discipline of the Church.

Pray that every child of the church may live and grow in the spirit of penitence.

v. The sacrifice of God is a troubled spirit.
r. A broken and a contrite heart, O God, Thou shalt not despise.

Let us pray

Lord, you raised St. Edward, King and Confessor, to govern and serve your people: may these ideals serve and flourish among us through his prayers.

Almighty and everlasting God, who hatest nothing that thou hast made and dost forgive the sins of all them that are penitent: create and make in us new and contrite hearts, that we worthily lamenting our sins, and acknowledging our wretchedness, may obtain of Thee, the God of all mercy, perfect remission and forgiveness; through Jesus Christ our Lord. **Amen.**

9. Before the Altar of Our Lady

The Magnificat

My soul doth magnify the Lord: and my spirit hath rejoiced in God my Saviour.
For he hath regarded: the lowliness of his handmaiden.
For behold, from henceforth: all generations shall call me blessed.
For he that is mighty hath magnified me: and holy in his name.
And his mercy is on them that fear him: throughout all generations.

He hath showed strength with his arm: he hath scattered the proud in the imagination of their hearts.
He hath put down the mighty from their seat: and hath exalted the humble and meek.
He hath filled the hungry with good things: and the rich he hath sent empty away.
He remembering his mercy: hath helped his servant Israel;
As he promised to our forefathers: Abraham and his seed, for ever.
Glory be to the Father, and to the Son: and to the Holy Spirit;
As it was in the beginning, is now, and ever shall be: world without end. **Amen.**

Contemplate in awe and wonder the mystery of the Holy Incarnation.

Pray that the Welsh Church may ever be true to the Faith, once delivered to the Saints.

Pray that all her members may believe rightly the Incarnation of Our Lord Jesus Christ.

v. The Angel said unto Mary
r. Hail, thou that art highly favoured:
blessed art thou among women.

Let us pray

We beseech thee, O Lord, pour thy grace into our hearts—that as we have known the Incarnation of Thy Son, Jesus Christ, by the message of an angel, so by his cross and passion we may be brought to the glory of his resurrection: through the same Jesus Christ our Lord. **Amen.**

or *The Angelus*

v. The Angel of the Lord brought tidings to Mary.
r. And she conceived by the Holy Ghost.
Hail Mary, full of grace, the Lord is with thee.
Blessed art thou among women and blessed is the fruit of thy womb Jesus.
Holy Mary, Mother of God, pray for us sinners now and at the hour of our death. **Amen.**

v. Behold the handmaid of the Lord.
r. Be it unto me according to thy Word.
Hail Mary etc.

v. And the Word was made flesh.
r. And dwelt amongst us.
Hail Mary etc.

v. Pray for us O holy Mother of God.
r. That we may be made worthy of the promises of Christ.

We beseech thee, O Lord, pour thy grace into our hearts; that as we have known the Incarnation of thy Son Jesus Christ by the message of an angel, so by his cross and passion we may be brought unto the glory of his resurrection; through the same Jesus Christ our Lord. **Amen.**

10. In the Chapel of St. Nicholas—A thanksgiving for children

Reading Mark 9: 32-36

Jesus asked his disciples 'What were you talking about on the way here?' They kept quiet however, because their talk had been a dispute as to who should be first. So he sat down and called the twelve to him, and this is what he said: 'If you want to be first, you must become the last of all, and the servant of all the others.' Then he took a child and brought him in among them. He put his arms round him and embraced him and then he said: 'Receive such a child as this in my name, and you welcome me; and in welcoming me you receive him by whom I am sent.'

Service of Penance

We are often blind to the wealth God offers us in life.

v. For the times when we have forgotten that children are our responsibility to train and help and love,
r. Lord, forgive us.
v. For the times when we have not realised that our own growth is tied up with what we do for children,
r. Lord, forgive us.

v. For the times when we reject children for their interfering with what we consider the real business of life,
r. Lord, forgive us.
v. For the times when we have been unaware of all that they can teach us of relationship with God,
r. Lord, forgive us.

Bidding Prayer

Let us put the needs of all children before you and ask your blessing on them and all who have dealings with children.

Help us to accept with understanding the teaching of the way of a child.

Keep children of all ages from evil—may there always be some grown man or woman to give them support.

Bless those who have no children of their own that they may find joy in working in some way for them.

Keep us in our own homes alive to the riches that come to us from our children.

Let us pray.

Almighty God, you use all creation to lead us to you, let us learn from little children how to draw near to you, our Father in heaven. **Amen.**

For the Youth of Wales

O God, we ask that we/they may follow in the footsteps of our Patron Saint, David, that like him we/they may be proud to live Christian lives in this country of Wales, to grow up to be active, responsible citizens, so that we/they may contribute our/their full part to the life of our/their country. This we ask in the name of Jesus Christ. **Amen.**

St. Nicholas: pray for us.

11. In the Chapel of St. Andrew

Remember all, who in their lives and by their deaths have borne witness to Jesus Christ in our Principality, and in this Cathedral.

Remember all, who are now preaching the Gospel of Christ, and are ministering the Sacraments.

Remember all, who day by day are seeking to confess Christ as their Master.

Pray that we may be strengthened by the Power of the Holy Spirit.

Pray that we may have the sense of the Divine Presence.

Pray that the Holy Angels may have us in their charge.

Pray for those who gave their lives in World Wars I and II.

v. Behold I see the Heavens opened:
r. And the Son of man standing on the right hand of God.

Let us pray
Almighty God, who didst give such grace unto Thy holy Apostle Saint Andrew, that he readily obeyed the calling of Thy Son Jesus Christ, and followed him without delay: grant unto us all, that we, being called by Thy holy word, may forthwith give up ourselves obediently to fulfil Thy holy commandments; through the same Jesus Christ our Lord. **Amen.**

Prayer for Peace

Lead me from Death to Life
from Falsehood to Truth

Lead me from Despair to Hope
from Fear to Trust

Lead me from Hate to Love
from War to Peace

Let Peace fill our Heart
our World, our Universe.

Peace Peace Peace

12. Chapel of Thomas A Becket—A Visit to The Blessed Sacrament

Pilgrimages can be very busy. When possible, find time for quiet in Our Lord's presence. Here are some prayers which may be useful.

Lord Jesus:
You alone are the Food
for eternity,
and you alone;
you alone can satisfy
the soul of man,
and you alone.

Jesus Christ,
close beside me here and now
yesterday, today and for ever

the same now as with Mary in Nazareth
the same as with Peter in Bethany,
You will not force yourself upon me
waiting for me to make the first step
waiting till I in turn ask you to come.
Jesus Christ
Jesus, Lord of all,
Christ, the Son of the Living God.

To whom shall we go?
You have the words of Eternal Life.
I believe in you
I love you
I trust you
I want you
I give myself to you.
Give yourself to me:
come Lord Jesus, come quickly.

O Lord Jesus Christ,
take as your right
receive as my gift
all my liberty
my memory, my understanding, my will
all that I have
all that I am
all that I can be.

To you, O Lord, I restore it,
all is yours
dispose of it according to your will
give me your love
give my your grace
it is enough for me.

Thanks be to you, Lord Jesus Christ
for all the benefits which you have given me
for all the pains and insults which you have borne for me.
O most merciful redeemer, friend and brother
may I know you more clearly
love you more dearly
and follow you more nearly day by day. **Amen.**

Soul of Christ, sanctify me.
Body of Christ, save me.
Blood of Christ, inebriate me.
Water from the side of Christ, wash me.
Passion of Christ, strengthen me.
O good Jesu, hear me,
Within thy wounds hide me,
Suffer me not to be separated from thee,
From the malicious enemy defend me,
In the house of my death call me,
And bid me come to thee,
That with thy saints I may praise thee for ever and ever.
Amen.

Lord, I believe in you: increase my faith.
I trust in you: strengthen my trust.
I love you: let me love you more and more.
I am sorry for my sins: deepen my sorrow.

I worship you as my first beginning,
I long for you as my last end,
I praise you as my constant helper,
and call on you as my loving protector.

Guide me by your wisdom,
correct me with your justice,
comfort me with your mercy,
protect me with your power.

I offer you, Lord, my thoughts: to be fixed on you;
my words: to have you for their theme;
my actions: to reflect my love for you:
my sufferings: to be endured for your greater glory.

I want to do what you ask of me:
in the way you ask,
for as long as you ask,
because you ask it,

Lord, enlighten my understanding,
strengthen my will,
purify my heart,
and make me holy.

Help me to repent of my past sins
and to resist temptation in the future.
Help me to rise above my human weaknesses
and to grow stronger as a Christian.

Let me love you, my Lord and my God,
and see myself as I really am:
a pilgrim in this world,
a Christian called to respect and love
all whose lives I touch,
those in authority over me
or those under my authority,
my friends and my enemies.

Help me conquer anger with gentleness,
greed by generosity,
apathy by fervour.
Help me to forget myself
and reach out towards others.

Make me prudent in planning,
courageous in taking risks.
Make me patient in suffering,
unassuming in prosperity.

Keep me, Lord, attentive at prayer,
temperate in food and drink,
diligent in my work,
firm in my good intentions.

Let my conscience be clear,
my conduct without fault,
my speech blameless,
my life well-ordered.

Put me on my guard against my human weakness.
Let me cherish your love for me,
keep your law,
and come at last to your salvation.

Teach me to realise that this world is passing,
that my true future is the happiness of heaven,
that life on earth is short,
and the life to come eternal.

Help me to prepare for death
with a proper fear of judgment,
but a greater trust in your goodness.
Lead me safely through death
to the endless joy of heaven.

Canticle

We believe:
God is spirit: and they that worship him must
worship him in spirit and in truth.
God is light: and if we walk in the light, as
he is in the light, we have fellowship one with
another.
God is love: and every one that loveth is born
of God and knoweth God.
Jesus is the Son of God: and God hath given to
us eternal life, and this life is in his Son.
We are children of God: and he hath given us
of his spirit.
If we confess our sins: he is faithful and just
to forgive us our sins.
The world passeth away and the lust thereof:
but he that doeth the will of God abideth for ever. **Amen.**

Eastern Orthodox Prayer

Set our hearts on fire with love to thee, O Christ Our God, that in that flame we may love thee with all our hearts, with all our mind, with all our soul, and with all our strength, and our neighbours as ourselves; so that, keeping thy commandments, we may glorify thee, the giver of all good gifts.

THE FOUR FEAST PILGRIMAGES TO ST. DAVID'S

D. Calendis Martii.	*On the kalends of the month*
For calaind mis Marta	*of March—not haughty are*
nit mordai ſna ngudi,	*they at prayer to them—*
Senan, Moinenn, Moisi,	*Senan, Moinenn, Moses, David*
Dauid Cille Muni.	*of Cell Muini.*

The Martyrology of Oengus the Culdee, Irish Church c.A.D. 800

These prayers and readings are for use, at choice, at any of the Stations, on the four feast days.

SAINT DAVID'S DAY MARCH 1st

Reading Rhygyfarch's Life of Saint David

The holy father David prescribed an austere system of monastic observance, requiring every monk to toil daily at manual labour and to lead a common life. So with unflagging zeal they work with hand and foot, they put the yoke to their own shoulders, and in their own holy hands, they bear the tools for labour in the fields. So by their own strength they procure every necessity for the community, while refusing possessions and detesting riches. They make no use of oxen for ploughing. Everyone is rich to himself and to the brethren, every man is his own ox.

When the field work is done they return to the enclosure of the monastery, to pass their time till evening at reading, writing, or in prayer. Then when the signal is heard for evening prayer everyone leaves what he is at and in silence, without an idle conversation, they make their way to church. When, with heart and voice attuned, they have completed the psalmody, they remain on their knees until stars appearing in the heaven bring day to its close; yet when all have gone, the father remains there alone making his own private prayer for the well-being of the church.

Shedding daily abundance of tears, offering daily his sweet-scented sacrifice of praise, aglow with an intensity of love, he consecrated with pure hands with fitting oblation of the Lord's body, and so, at the conclusion of the morning offices, attained alone to the converse of angels. Then the whole day was spent undaunted and untired, in teaching, praying, on his knees, caring for the brethren, and for orphans and children, and widows, and everyone in need, for the weak and the sick, for travellers and in feeding many. The rest of this stern way of life would be profitable to imitate, but the shortness of this account forbids our entering upon it, but in every way his life was ordered in imitation of the monks of Egypt.

Response Ps. 36: 4 Ps. 88: 19, 20

r. I have found David, my servant, and with my holy oil anointed him. I will grant his heart's desire.
v. I have exalted one chosen from the people.
I will grant his heart's desire.

Collect

Lord God, who called the people of Wales to the glorious light of the Gospel through the cheerful example of Saint David, grant that supported by his prayer we may grow in grace and in the knowledge of our Lord, Jesus Christ, Your Son, Who lives and reigns with you and the Holy Spirit, God, for ever and ever.

Prayer

Almighty God, favourably regard the sacrifices of praise and the devout prayers which we present to thee in honour of thy blessed confessor and bishop, David; and what our own merit may not obtain may thy mercy and his frequent intercession for us effect. Through . . .
Secret prayer from the MS. Vespesian A. *Mass of Saint David*

NATIVITY OF SAINT JOHN THE BAPTIST
JUNE 24th

Reading Acts 13: 23-25

Of this man's posterity God has brought to Israel a Saviour, Jesus, as he promised.
Before his coming John had preached a baptism of repentance to all the people of Israel. And as John was finishing his course, he said, 'What do you suppose that I am? I am not he. No, but after me one is coming, the sandals of whose feet I am not worthy to untie.'

Bidding

Give us, O God, something of the spirit of your servant, John the Baptist,
His moral courage,
His contentment with simplicity,
His refusal to be fettered by this world,
His faithfulness in witness to the end.

So may we be heralds of Christ and his kingdom and make ready his way, to the glory of his name. **Amen.**

Response

God our Father, you chose John the Baptist to announce the kingdom of Christ to all men.
Joyfully we pray, therefore:

r. Lord, guide us in the way of peace.

Even in his mother's womb you chose John to prepare the way for your Son; give us the faith to know Christ, and to make Him known.

r. Lord, guide us in the way of peace.

You inspired the Baptist to recognize the Lamb of God: through us, let the world recognize your Son, our Lord, Jesus Christ.

r. **Lord, guide us in the way of peace.**

You disposed your prophet to give way before Christ: give us the humility to let his light shine in the world.

r. Lord, guide us in the way of peace.

You called John even to die for you; grant that we may share his burning zeal for the truth.

r. Lord, guide us in the way of peace.
Remember the dead who have walked in the path of life: bring them to new life, cleansed from all stain of sin.

r. Lord, guide us in the way of peace.

Our Father . . .

Almighty God and Father, you sent John the Baptist to the people of Israel to make them ready for Christ the Lord. Give us the grace of Joy in the Spirit, and guide the hearts of all the faithful in the way of salvation and peace.
(We make our prayer) through our Lord.

SAINT MICHAEL AND ALL ANGELS
SEPTEMBER 29th

A Reading from the homilies of St. Gregory the Great on the Gospels.

It must be realised that the word 'angel' is the name of an office, and not of a nature. For these holy spirits of our homeland in heaven are always spirits, but in no way can they always be called 'angels' or 'messengers' since they are angels only when something is announced through them. Those who make minor announcements are called angels, those who make important ones are called archangels.

Hence it is that not just any angel was sent to the Virgin Mary but that Gabriel the archangel was sent: it was right that the proper one for this role should be of the highest rank of angels since he was to announce the greatest news of all.

Angels are known by proper names as well, to indicate their powers and their work. In that holy city where perfect knowledge is derived from the vision of Almighty God, if proper names are assigned to them it is not that their persons could not be identified without names. But when angels come to minister to us, even the names by which we know them are taken from their ministry—Michael means 'Who is like God', Gabriel 'Strength of God', Raphael 'Healing of God'.

Whenever a mighty deed is in question, Michael is assigned, so that by his actions and name it may be made known that no one can do what God can do. So in the case of our ancient enemy, who in his pride wanted to be like God when he said: 'I will ascend to heaven; above the stars of God I will set my throne on high; I will make myself like the Most High': when he is shown to be condemned to eternal punishment at the end of the world, he is described as about to do battle with Michael, as Saint John says: 'War broke out with Michael the Archangel'.

Gabriel was sent to Mary, for Gabriel means 'Strength of God'. He came to announce him who deigned to be lowly so as to wage war on the spiritual powers of air. He who came as God of power and as one strong in battle was to be announced by Gabriel, the strength of God.

Finally Raphael is interpreted, as we have said, as 'Healing of God', since he wiped away the shadows of blindness from Tobias when he touched his eyes to cure him. The one who is sent to cure, was indeed worthy of the name 'Healing of God'.

Response

An angel stood at the altar of the temple having a golden censer in his hand, and a great quantity of incense was given to him; and from the angel's hand the smoke of the incense went up in the presence of God.
A thousand thousand waited on him, ten thousand times ten thousand stood before him, and from the angel's hand the smoke of the incense went up in the presence of God.

Father, as you laid the foundation of creation, the stars of the morning sang for joy, and the sons of God in chorus chanted your praise.

r. All you spirits, worship the Lord.

Lord, your heavenly servants were sent to men to guard and lead them. Keep us faithful to your call today.
r. All you spirits, worship the Lord.

Lord, the angels stand before your throne to praise you. Help us to seek your face to-day.
r. All you spirits, worship the Lord.

Lord, your sons are called to be like angels of light. Keep us pure in heart and body.
r. All you spirits, worship the Lord.

Lord, we thank you for your glorious power; we praise your victory over the powers of darkness; for yours is the kingdom, the power, and the glory, for all ages to come.

Our Father

Lord God of hosts, in your all-wise plan you assign to angels and to men the services they have to render you. Grant that the angels who adore you in heaven, may protect us here on earth. Through Jesus Christ our Lord.

Extra Reading

Scripture refers to the direct ministry of angels much that we attribute to the 'laws of nature'. The wind, the cloud, the fire, the pestilence, the stroke of death, perhaps the very virtue of healing waters, are assigned to the action of personal beings, whose presence has been openly shown from time to time to assure our faith . . . Scripture tells us that messengers of God are about us on every side. The ministry of angels is the perfected type of our work. Are they the messengers of God? So are we, charged to declare one to another the truth we know. Are they the sons of God? So are we, by the power which Christ has given us. Are they called the 'watchers'? Such is the charge which the Lord has laid upon us. Are they called the 'holy ones'? Such is the character which we are commended to secure. Do they fulfil the will of God faithfully, cheerfully, perfectly? Day by day we pray that we may do that will on earth as they do it in heaven.

B. F. Westcott Village Sermons

A Sequence for St. Michael and All Angels

Michael, Archangel
Of the King of Kings,
Give ear to our voices.

We acknowledge thee to be the Prince of the citizens of heaven:
And at thy prayer God sends
His angels unto men,

That the enemy with cunning craft shall not prevail
To do the hurt he craves
To weary men.
Yea, thou hast the dominion of perpetual Paradise,
And ever do the holy angels honour thee.

Thou wert seen in the Temple of God,
A censer of gold in thy hands,
And the smoke of it fragranat with spices
Rose up till it came before God.

Thou with strong hand didst smite the cruel dragon,
And many souls didst rescue from his jaws.
Then there was a great silence in heaven,
And a thousand thousand saying "Glory to the Lord King".

Hear us, Michael,
Greatest angel,
Come down a little
From thy high seat,
To bring us the strength of God,
And the lightening of His mercy.

And do thou, Gabriel,
Lay low our foes,
And thou, Raphael,
Heal our sick,
Purge our disease, ease thou our pain,
And give us to share
In the joys of the blessed.

Alcuin.

Thou Michael of
militance
Thou Michael of wounding,
shield me from the grudge
of ill wishers this night,
ill wishes this night.

O Angel
guardian
of my right hand
attend thou me
this night.

Rescue thou me
in the battling floods,
array me in thy linen,
for I am naked.

Succour me,
for I am feeble and
forlorn.

Steer thou
my coracle in the
crooked eddies,

Guide thou
my step in gap and in pit,
guard thou me
in the
treacherous turnings,

and save thou me from
the scaith of the wicked,

save thou me
from scaith this night.

Drive thou from me,
the taint of pollution,
ecompass thou me
till doom
from evil,

O kindly angel of
my right hand,
deliver thou me
from the wicked this night.

Deliver thou me
this night.

ALL SAINT OF WALES NOVEMBER 8th

Reading from an unknown Welsh Author, 12th Century

The praise of God at the beginning and in the end, He does not reject, He does not refuse him who attempts it—the only Son of Mary, the lord of princes; He will come like the sun, from the east to the north. Mary Mother of Christ, glory of maidens, intercede in Thy great mercy with Thy Son to cast out our sins. God be above us, God before us, God who rules, the Lord of Heaven, may he give us a share of mercy. O Lordly-hearted One, may there be peace between us without rejection, and may I make amends for all the sins I have committed. Before going to my tomb, to my green grave, in the darkness without candle to my grave-mound, to my recess, to my hiding-place, to my repose, after horses and trolling the pale mead, and carousal, and consort with women, I shall not sleep, I will take thought for my end. We are in a world of grievous wantonness, like leaves from the treetops it will pass away. Woe to the miser who amasses great wealth, and unless he devotes it to God, though he be suffered in the course of this world, there will be peril at his end. The fool knows not in his heart how to tremble, he does not rise early, he does not pray, he does not keep vigil, he does not chant prayers, he does not crave mercy; pride and arrogance and pomp, bitterly will they be paid for in the end. He plumps his body but for toads and snakes and lions, and practises iniquity; but Death will come in through the door and ravenously it will gather him up and carry him off. Old age and infirmity of mind draw nigh, your hearing, your sight, your teeth are failing, the skin of your fingers becomes wrinkled, old age and grey hairs do this to you. May Michael intercede for us with the Lord of Heaven for a shore of mercy.

May-time, fairest season, noisy are the birds, green the woods, the ploughs are in the furrow, the ox in the yoke, green is the sea, the lands grow many-coloured. When the cuckoos sing on the tops of the splendid trees my wretchedness grows greater; the smoke is painful, my distress is manifest since my kinsmen have passed away. On hill, in dale, in the islands of the sea, in every way one goes, there is no seclusion from the blessed Christ. My Friend, my Intercessor, it was my desire to attain the Land far away to which Thou wentest. Seven and seven score and seven hundred saints have gone to the one Tribunal, and in the presence of the Blessed Christ they have not endured terror. The gift I ask, may it not be denied me, peace between me and God; may I find the road to the Gate of Glory, Christ, may I not be sad before Thy throne.

Bidding

Lord God Almighty, you alone are holy, and we see your holiness reflected in the lives of your saints. Let us live, serving you in holiness and justice.

Lord our God, we proclaim your greatness at all times.
May we be worthy sons, living lives of true service.

Lord, you filled your saints with the Holy Spirit,
so that they might lead your people with prudence and love.
Give all leaders a share in that Spirit,
so that they may bring your people to you.

Lord Jesus, you called brother, sister and mother
those who do the will of your Father.
We pray that we may always do what pleases the Father.

Our Father

Almighty God, who dost call thine elect from every nation, and dost show forth thy glory in their lives: grant that we, following the example of the Saints of Wales and strengthened by their fellowship, may be fruitful in good works to the glory of thy Name; through Jesus Christ our Lord. **Amen.**

or Almighty, ever-living God,
who in the lives of the saints
continually give us new proofs of your love:
lead us to the faithful imitation of Christ,
by the help of their prayer and the spur of their example.
(We make our prayer) through our Lord. **Amen.**

Prayer for the Province of Wales

Almighty God, who by the power of thy Holy Spirit didst send forth thine apostles to make disciples of all nations, and to baptize them into thy Church: quicken, we beseech thee, by the same spirit, the Church in Wales, that with wisdom and fervent zeal we may continue to preach thy Gospel, till all are brought into the clear light and true knowledge of thee and of thy Son, Jesus Christ our Lord. **Amen.**

A EUCHARIST FOR PILGRIMS

Introit

Be thou my strong rock, and house of defence:
that thou mayest save me. For thou art my strong
rock and my castle: be thou also my guide, and
lead me for thy name's sake.

ps. In thee, O Lord, have I put my trust, let me never be put to confusion, deliver me in thy righteousness.

Collect

Assist us, O Lord, in these our supplications, and dispose the way of thy servants (N. and N.) towards the attainment of thy salvation; that among all the changes and chances of their journey through this life, they may be ever defended by thy help. Through the merits of thy Son Jesus Christ our Lord. **Amen.**

Lesson Gen. 24: 7

The Lord, the God of heaven, who took me from my father's house and from the land of my birth, and who spoke to me and swore to me, 'To your descendants I will give this land', he will send his angel before you.

Epistle 2 Cor. 11: 19

You gladly bear with fools, being wise yourselves! For you bear it if a man makes slaves of you, or preys upon you, or takes advantage of you, or puts on airs, or strikes you in the face. To my shame, I must say, we were too weak for that! But whatever any one dares to boast of—I am speaking as a fool—I also dare to boast of that. Are they Hebrews? So am I. Are they Israelites? So am I. Are they descendants of Abraham? So am I. Are they servants of Christ? I am a better one —I am talking like a madman—with far greater labours, far more imprisonments, with countless beatings, and often near death. Five times I have received at the hands of the Jews the forty lashes less one. Three times I have been beaten with rods; once I was stoned. Three times I have been shipwrecked; a night and a day I have been adrift at sea; on frequent journeys, in danger from rivers, danger from robbers, danger from my own people, danger from Gentiles, danger in the city, danger in the wilderness, danger at sea, danger from false brethren; in toil and hardship, through many a sleepless night, in hunger and thirst, often without food, in cold and exposure. And, apart from other things, there is the daily pressure upon me of my anxiety for all the churches. Who is weak, and I am not weak? Who is made to fall, and I am not indignant? If I must boast, I will boast of the things that show my weakness. The God and Father of the Lord Jesus, he who is blessed for ever, knows that I do not lie.

Gradual

v. Be thou my strong rock and house of defence: that thou mayest save me.
r. In thee, O Lord have I put my trust: let me never be put to confusion.
v. Be thou my strong rock and house of defence: that thou mayest save me.
r. Alleluya. Ye that fear the Lord, put your trust in the Lord; he is their helper and defender.

Gospel Matt. 10: 7-15

Preach as you go, saying, 'The kingdom of heaven is at hand'. Heal the sick, raise the dead, cleanse lepers, cast out demons. You received without paying, give without pay. Take no gold, nor silver, nor copper in your belts, no bag for your journey, nor two tunics, nor sandals, nor a staff; for the laborer deserves his food. And whatever town or village you enter, find out who is worthy in it, and stay with him until you depart. As you enter the house, salute it. And if the house is worthy, let your peace come upon it; but if it is not worthy, let your peace return to you. And if any one will not receive you or listen to your words, shake off the dust from your feet as you leave that house or town. Truly, I say to you, it shall be more tolerable on the day of judgement for the land of Sodom and Gomorrah than for that town.

Offertory Prayer

And all they that know thy name will put their trust in thee; for thou, Lord, has never failed them that seek thee.
O praise the Lord which dwelleth in Sion, for he forgetteth not the complaint of the poor. *In Easter-tide:* Alleluya

Post Communion Prayer

We beseech thee, O Lord, that the reception of the sacrament of the heavenly mystery may further the good success of thy servants' journey, and bring them to all things profitable to their salvation. Through Jesus Christ, our Lord. **Amen.**

After the Holy Eucharist the priest may say the following prayers over the pilgrims either kneeling or prostrate before the altar, whether they be on the threshold of their pilgrimage or about to return from the holy place.

v. The Lord be with you.
r. And with thy spirit.

Let us pray

O God of infinite mercy and boundless majesty, whom neither space nor time separate from those whom you love, be present with thy servants who everywhere put their trust in thee and vouchsafe to be their leader and companion in every way in which they shall go. Let no adversity harm them, no difficulty hinder them, let all things be healthful and all things prosperous for them; that whatsoever they shall rightly ask, they may speedily and effectually obtain by the aid of thy right hand. Through Jesus Christ our Lord. **Amen.**

Let us pray

May the almighty and everlasting God, who is the way, the truth and the life, dispose your journey according to his good pleasure; may he send his angel Raphael to be your guardian in your pilgrimage; to lead you on your way, in peace, to the place where you wish to go, and bring you back again in safety on your return to us. May Mary, the blessed Mother of Jesus, pray for you together with all angels and archangels and patriarchs and prophets. The holy apostles Peter and Paul pray for you together with the confessors, and virgins; and may the saints, whose prayers you ask, together with all the saints in heaven obtain for you just desires, and prosperity, and remission of all sins, and life everlasting. Through our Lord and Saviour, Jesus Christ our Lord. **Amen.**

The pilgrims then depart in the Name of the Lord.

THE PROPER OF THE MASS OF SAINT DAVID: ANCIENT WELSH MANUAL MISSAL TEXT c. 1440

Introit

Let us all rejoice in the Lord, as we keep the feast in honour of Saint David the bishop: on whose solemnity the Angels rejoice, and praise together the Son of God.

Ps. Lord, remember David: and all his meekness.

On the Commemoration of Saint David

Introit:

The Lord made to him a covenant of peace, and made him a prince; that the dignity of priesthood should be to him for ever. *In Eastertide:* Alleluya, alleluya.

Ps. O Lord, remember David: and all his meekness.
v. Glory be to the Father.

Collect

O God who didst foretell thy blessed confessor and bishop, David, by the message of an angel thirty years before his birth: we beseech thee by his intercession, whose memory we are keeping, we may attain to eternal joy. Through . . .

Lesson from the Book of Wisdom

The author of Ecclesiasticus sings the praises of a whole group of Old Testament figures: Enoch, Abraham, Isaac, Jacob, Moses and Aaron. The bishops have replaced them as leaders of the people of God. The greatness of all of them is derived from the priesthood of Christ of whom the first named were the figures and the bishops the continuation in the fullness of time.

Noe Behold, a great priest, who in his days pleased God, and was found just: and in the time of wrath he was made a reconciliation. *Abraham* There was not found the like to him who kept the law of the Most High. Therefore by an oath the Lord made him to increase among his people. *Isaac* He gave him the blessing of all nations, and confirmed His covenant upon his head. He acknowledged him in His blessings; He preserved for him His mercy; and he found grace before the eyes of the Lord. *Moses* He glorified him in the sight of kings, and gave him a crown of glory. *Aaron* He made an everlasting covenant with him, and gave him a great priesthood: and made him blessed in glory. To execute the office of the priesthood, and to have praise in His name, and to offer him a worthy incense for an odour of sweetness.

Gradual

Lord, thou hast prevented him with the blessing of goodness: thou hast set upon his head a crown of precious stones.

v. He asked life and thou gavest him length of days for ever and ever. Alleluya.

v. I have found David my servant: with my holy oil have I annointed him. Alleluya.

Sequence

David the faithful witness of the New Law, like a bright star from heaven, shines forth in Britannia;
His most illustrious life and true teaching adorn Menevia.
Like the birth of the Forerunner, the Baptist, so was this bishop divinely foretold.
The future greatness of Christ's servant is declared by heavenly signs: honey, water and mystic hind.
This is the champion of the Britanni, the leader and teacher of the Welsh, supporting the citizens of God.
Single-hearted he condemns luxury; spurning the city, he seeks the vale befitting the lowly.
At his birth the people name him 'Dewi ddyfrwr', which means 'David of the aquatic life'.
He cures the blind, he expels diseases; the Gospel Psalmist drives forth the devil, putting him to flight.
A doctor of (Christ's) law, he writes a volume, which the hand of God completes with golden letter.

O David our leader, thou strong champion, do thou also overcome by thy prayers Goliath, the enemy of our earthly course.

Gospel Mark 13: 33-37

(At that time: Jesus said unto his disciples:) 'Take heed, watch, for you do not know when the time will come. It is like a man going on a journey, when he leaves home and puts his servants in charge, each with his work, and commands the doorkeeper to be on the watch. Watch therefore —for you do not know when the master of the house will come, in the evening, or at midnight, or at cockcrow, or in the morning—lest he come suddenly and find you asleep. And watch I say to you, I say to all: Watch.'

Offertory Prayer

I have found David my servant: and with holy oil have I anointed him, my hand shall hold him fast: and my arm shall strengthen him. *In Eastertide:* Alleluya.

Secret Prayer

Almighty God, favourably regard the sacrifices of praise and the devout prayers which we present to thee in honour of thy blessed confessor and bishop, David; and what our own merit may not obtain may thy mercy and his frequent intercession for us effect. Through . . .

Communion Prayer

Blessed is that servant whom the Lord when he cometh shall find watching: verily I say unto you, He shall make him ruler over all (his) gods. *In Eastertide:* Alleluya, alleluya.

Post-Communion Prayer

We who are satisfied with the sacred gift beseech thee, O Lord, that him whom we now know by sure faith beneath a sacrament we may, through the intercession of blessed David thy confessor and bishop, behold with unclouded vision face to face in heaven. Through the same . . .

AN ANTHOLOGY OF POEMS, PRAYERS AND HYMNS FOR PILGRIMS

Dyfed

I speak from deep in Dyfed, little Wales
beyond both Wales and England, where like snails
upon the sea's green leaf the shells and sails

of ships of saints once bustled in the bays,
busy as bees about their lawful ways,
all raising up a honeycomb of praise;

from Dyfed where Pryderi used to ride
and rule the seven green cantrefs; where beside
his bay Giraldus watched the lawn-sleeved tide

fawn on his castle piers at Manorbier,
and sighed, and rode off for another year
to Rome to gain the Holy Father's ear.

I speak from Dyfed, Wales within Wales, world
within world, within whose heart lay curled
the flower from which Four Branches were unfurled—

a green and mighty myth where princes pass
and galleys glide as on a sea of glass,
and poetry the wind that stirs the grass.

Raymond Garlick

Intimations

We have no certainty the soul but dreams
When it arises far above this life,
Above man's journey from the cradle to the grave,
Whispering of things that words will not reveal
Though we may force them far beyond their limits
Like stars into the vast eternal space.

Has not the soul a story of its own?

A dark ebb strangely murmurs in its depths
On distant shores we cannot reach, on shores
Where Memory was lost in wrecks stupendous
Of some great world or worlds.

Are the stars above
As splendid and divine as poets sing?
Their power sublime on our responding spirit
May it not be the hold of memories dim
Of far diviner scenes, radiant of God?
The stars are in us! And all poetry
Is but the recollection of our past,
Or premonition of what we shall be.

What mortal man lives now who never feels
The sudden spin of a long forgotten world
Flashing across his path, strangely familiar,
Or brushing the tip of a long promontory of memories?

Our imaginings, who can
Prove or disprove they are the fragments strewn
On a deep sea, the wreck of a nobler life,
And that the soul in stupor lies, until
Restored by the ever-seeking, living breath
Of poetry? O blessed hour, when God
Appears, a Sun in Majesty above
Earth's many days, and the Holy Spirit's path
A ray of light on the world's broken tracks
Lighting the way back to those heights Divine!

Islwyn (William Thomas, 1832-78)
translated from the Welsh by D. M. Lloyd

The Church

When the stars weigh heavily upon our flesh,
And their antiquity fills us with dread,
She rears a fort where our impoverished
Spirit can flee, come night, and bow its head;
And that is where we set down at your feet
The burden of our sinful pettiness,
The humble frailty of our flesh and blood,
And terror of your wondrous universe.
But from Your hand as from a tranquil fountain
Each form of what exists we see, descends,
We see Your back is in the deepest ocean,
Your shoulders, in the firmness of the stones,
The heavens countless stars and nebulae
Only Your cloak of immortality.

Gwenallt. 1899-1968

Seal Island

seal-curved sleeping island
grey-skinned under channel wind

from your glistening back trees
bracken giant ferns rise

above the red and white Monastery
nestling in deep skin-folds

surrounded by gulls, you bask
eyes shut, frozen to stone

yet we half expect you to slide
oil-smooth over rocks vanishing
under green Atlantic waves.

Alison Bielski

St. David's Cathedral

Eight hundred years the stones
Have borne attendance on Majesty
Here in this echoing House:
Stones from the cliff foot,
Wrought and hammered by a million years
Of sea and hurricane,
Cut and tooled in skilful pride
For vault and moulding.

Hallowed, time moved in them
As prayers ascended, and the rain
Beat its pattern
      on the cloud-cold roof and aisles
Stripped of their covering
      through wanton years.

Eyes that measured time, and hands
      honed by toil
Are irrecoverable dust;
And yet,
      while this House stands
Not wholly can they die
      who built it:

Within the stillness of a summer day
A shaft of sunlight will
      with gold
Burnish afresh each shadowed arch,
Tracing its curve
      as once
Some mason traced it with his
      dreaming eye,
And it will stand afresh against the dark,
His living testament.

Mary Denyer

St. David's Cathedral

Austerely beautiful it stands
In this green-bastioned glen,
The jewel of the fabled Western land
Beyond the haunts of men;
For here the Norman Leia dreamed and planned,
Building this massive nave,
Pier, arch and architrave,
With skilled, unerring hand,
Of purple stone that knew the shock and roar
Of thundering seas upon the fortressed shore;
And here the Western Wykeham, Gower, wrought
With sure, consumate art,
His chambered rood-screen, where, enmeshed and caught,
In sparkling cusp and crocket here
About his princely bier
And all the visions of a poet's heart.
And like an Oriental dream,
Above the high, triumphant nave is spread
Pole's rich, grey roof of fretted arch and beam,
Each gorgeous carven pendant overhead,
Like damask out of Araby,
While round about the thrusting lantern tower
Burn colour and red heraldry.

Without, stands Gower's palace in array
Of lordly halls and ageless, proud arcades,
Built in the soaring splendour of his prime,
Transfigured by the crafty hands of time
To mellow richness of sublime decay.
So from this place of beauty never fades
The glory of the builders, those who made
With pious, artist hands and heart aglow
This jewel of the fabled Western land,
In memory, long years ago,
Of one who lived and prayed
In this green-bastioned glen,
Saint David, Cymric Prince of Christian men.

A. G. Prys-Jones

Saint David's Day

By a rope across his nape, beneath his armpits,
The saint dragged a plough of wood, and broke the ground.
Then barefoot he would tramp the clods, the cant
Of the furrow beneath his sole a long delight.
God's zealous ox, his strength; his holy lust—
Husbandman of a nation's seasons on his strip.
He worked a stony tilth beneath the rock,
Made the slopes fertile and uprooted the thorns.
He sowed the seed that after death became
Christ's bread for thousands at the boards of grace.
Christ's scripture ornament was his rough headland,
A hard securing of the saint's beginnings.
If only after our swift ploughs we sowed
Today the grains his right hand smoothly spread.

Arms dump and aerodrome we have shared the saint's
  headland
And up above purrs a contented hell,
Its docile dancers underneath hard at it
Serving the voracious rows of teeth of steel.
Eternal tents of Mammon—here they take
My poor bemuddled folk into their plot,
The plaited paint entangling them like eels
And the easy craze of many in one spot.

Power of David, should it cross the heather as a tempest
The tents of Mammon would not be left standing on the
  field;
It would whirl their whole providence of puff and sham
And the proper claims of blood to streaming ribbons,
And the long insolence and pollution of the pound
Would dance the dried leaves' dance in the high wind.

Waldo Williams (1904-1971)

(The promontory of St. David's Head was taken over by the War Ministry in 1939)

At St. David's

There's no beyond. The world's end,
This bowl's pure rim, rock ridges
And hillcrest houses, firm arc
Sharp-etched on sheer blue absence.

Brimming, today, this chalice
On the westmost thrust of Wales
With sunblest air, clear and cool
As its saint's sole refreshment,
Cordial for two secular
Pilgrims pointing our progress
Through his land with this last day's
Bus-trip to a beginning.

Our descent into the font
Is unhurried. The hillside
Sprouts gravestones casually
As we pass, punctuating
The grass like the black cattle sprawled
Below, strewn on the meadow,
Mild with May, beyond the grey
Shell of the Bishop's Palace.
Dewi's House poses, mellowed,
Composite tombstone, by sun,
For our candid tourist eye.
Only the branch-benched synod
Of crows' incessant brangling
Discredits Pelagius.

Did David find such a day
A grace, I wonder, sunshine
A shadow of Paradise?
The stone fortress we enter
To admire the uphill nave,
Arcade, choir-screen, oak ceiling,
And pray for a safe trip home,

Then abandon for sunlight,
Commemorates Dewi's huts
Of daub and wattle, rigour
Of cold water, bread, and herbs.
Ascetic missionary,
He broke, yoke across shoulders,
Ground hard as the human heart,
Struck from the rock of this dell
A well of living water
To christen the soil of Wales.
Place to rest and be thankful
For wayfaring centuries,
Its tranquil benediction
Bathes us now, open-handed
Hospice, as we take our leave.

As we trudge the slow upwards
Slope within, back to its lip,
This bell swung, open-mouthed awe,
By David to God's glory,
We hear its cathedral tongue
Toll the close of our springtime
Sojourn in Wales. Unclouded
Afternoon. The sun has blessed
Us homewards. The hill's austere
Stones warn we may not return.

Joseph P. Clancy

St. David's Pilgrimage

Sea and sky before you lie,
this earth beneath your trusting feet, God lifted
from the Ocean bed marks clear the way.
In heritage of ancient days your Pilgrimage goes forth
vibrating to a song of known endeavour to quicken every
heart and mind.
These miriad years our Ancient Land has known
and Treasure made, we now absorb.

Holy, Holy, Holy Lord God of all these things, born
of thy Mighty Hand, whose shadow bright across our
present path, where all the saints, living still, lend
strength to faltering step and aching mind, whose
Truth all men shall know in courage of the Cross
so bravely born.

Here where our Path to seaward winds,
dark against the wild Atlantic surge, shapes as of men
in height quite other Saint David and St. Teilo stand.
Welcome to us they give, this day of March, as
memories' flames ride high his church to burn,
on land he Hallowed.

The Soul, the Spirit's Life, both His and ours
you can not so destroy, come build again, and yet again—
The truth these centuries have wrought, through
Lives long gone, lives on in us, footsteps line the
sacred path we take, St. David's way; within his long
endeavour beneath the glowing shadow of the Cross
we walk, Heads held High, the Golden light of Joy
within our Hearts,
O Nata Lux de Lumini.

For Father Brendan O'Malley *by Ray Howard Jones*

Saint David

Out of marvellous tales
And the legends told
Of Saint David of Wales
In cloister and cell
By those who extolled
His virtue and grace,
We have woven his spell
And have heard his voice
Like a silver bell
From missal and page
Limned bright with art,
And hallowed with age
He has come to our heart.

With the chorals of Spring
On the wind-blown plain
And the magic of meadows
Grown rich with rain,
With the earth that exults
In the conquering sun,
And Winter retreating
And blossoms begun;
With daffodils shaking
Their pennants of gold
And woodlands awaking,
He comes to his fold
To grant us his blessing
And the light of his face,
As he came long ago
In the dawn of our race.

A. G. Prys-Jones

A Song of the Pilgrim Road

The road to old St. David's
Is the white road of the blest,
The roving road which gave the vales
The pilgrims' songs, the palmers' tales
When all the wandering roads of Wales
Went winding to the West.

The road to old St. David's
Is a road of hills and sea,
A road where prelates, Lords and Kings
With peasants, chieftains, princelings,
Came humbly bearing offerings
To a cherished sanctuary.

The road to old St. David's
As famed as the road to Rome
Leads to the lone, sequestered place
Where David raised his house of grace,
And here the heart of an ancient race
Found hostelry and home.

The road to old St. David's
Is the road of the Saint who trod
Its first rough trackways to proclaim
The love of Christ, and lit the flame
Of faith which glories in the Name
And Fatherhood of God.

The road to old St. David's
In all its wandering ways
Remembers how from age to age
Folk came on pious pilgrimage
Seeking a nation's heritage,
And singing their songs of praise.

A. G. Prys-Jones

The Hermit

Alone in my little hut without a human being in my company, dear has been the pilgrimage before going to meet death.

A remote hidden little cabin, for forgiveness of my sins; a conscience upright and spotless before holy Heaven.

Making holy the body with good habits, treading it boldly down; weak tearful eyes for forgiveness of my desires.

Desires feeble and withered, renunciation of this poor world, clean live thoughts; this is how I would seek God's forgiveness.

Eager wailings to cloudy Heaven, sincere and truly devout confession, fervent showers of tears.

A cold, anxious bed, like the lying-down of the doomed, a brief apprehensive sleep, invocations frequent and early.

My food, my staple diet—it is a dear bondage—my meal would not make me full-blooded, without doubt.

Dry bread weighed out, well we bow the head; water of the fair-coloured hillside, that is the draught you should drink.

A bitter meagre meal, diligently feeding the sick, suppression of quarrelling and visiting, a calm serene conscience.

It would be desirable, a pure, holy blemish, cheeks dry and sunken, skin leathery and lean.

Treading the paths of the Gospel, singing psalms every Hour; and end of talking and long stories; constant bending of the knees.

My Creator to visit me, my Lord, my King, my spirit to seek Him in the eternal kingdom where He is.

Let this be the end of vice in the precincts of churches, a lovely little cell among many graves, and I alone there.

Alone in my little hut, all alone so, alone I came into the world, alone I shall go from it.

If being alone I have done wrong at all, through the pride of this world, hear my wail as I lament all alone, O God!

Eighth-Ninth Century Irish: author unknown

To the south of St. David's below Pembroke, lies the tiny Chapel of St. Govan. Wedged into the cliff on a precipitous headland, the chapel still evokes to-day the solitary life of the celtic saint who lived there.

The site is very ancient and dates back to the sixth century, although the present chapel was built some seven hundred years later. On the left through an arched doorway is a niche where Govan hid from his pagan persecutors, the rock miraculously opening and closing behind him. Anyone who turns around in the niche is supposed to be assured of luck.

Tradition has it that St. Govan lies buried under the altar. There is certainly a strong feeling of presence within this coastal chapel and it is not difficult to sense the retained interest of the Saint himself.

St. Govan

St. Govan, he built him a cell
By the side of the Pembroke sea,
And there, as the crannied sea-gulls dwell,
In a tiny, secert citadel
He sighed for eternity.

St. Govan, he built him a cell
Between the wild sky and the sea,
Where the sunsets redden the rolling swell
And brooding splendour has thrown her spell
On valley and moorland lea.

St. Govan still lies in his cell,
But his soul, long since, is free,
And one may wonder—and who can tell—
If good St. Govan likes Heaven as well
As his cell by that sounding sea?

A. G. Prys-Jones

St. Govan

Crossing from Wexford
through that barbarous sea
here you landed first,
preached, built and stayed.
Gobhan—smith, worker of men.

Why?—to bring the Light of Christ
to Lundy's pirates?
To succour the meek farmers of earth and water
they pressed upon?
Because, hounded like an otter,
you found a rock that split and closed
on you like a womb, slipping you free
after their angry going?

Later, stealing the silver bell
that tongued your calling inland
they drew the wrath of angels, lost the plunder
to a mysterious force which laid
its rich voice in rock, giving out song
to the blows of your staff. Was it
for such celestial tricks you held so long
to the cliff's sanctuary, raised a chapel?

Your holy well has dried, cures no blindness,
unbends no twisted bones;
what spirits clung to the place have flown,
though the mud floor is marked by the curious
descending the uncountable steps.

No, what held you is clear:
it was and is the sea.
The sea that bore you crashes
against the brittle cliffs,
breaks and smooths their jaggedness,
works into the bulk of the coast,
below dunes, far below the rasp of cannon-fire
tolling the unholy hour.

Tony Curtis

Dygŵyl Dewi

Holl enweirwyr mawr a man,
cenwch gân yn llafar,
fore Dygŵyl Dewi Sant,
dros holl blant y ddaear.
Nid oes odid un o fil
heddiw o hil Adda
nad yw'n wên i gyd ar wawr
dygwyl mawr pysgota.

Byddai Dewi'n wan ei fyd
adeg ympryd Grawys,
ac ymgosbai rhag ei drwyn
oll er mwyn Paradwys.
Byddai'n deffro yn y nos
agos a llewygu,
wedi gweled drwy ei hun
fochyn wedi'i fachu.

Ond gwrandawyd ar ei lef
gan y nef yn dirion;
gyrrwyd ugain brithyll brych
ato'n sych o'r afon.
Padell ffrio ar y tan
yn rhoi can y cinio,
a'r brithylliaid yn un rhes
ar y tes yn tisio.

Yna meddai Dewi Sant,
'Bwytawn gant ohonyn,
ac nid pechod yn y byd
ympryd mor amheuthun.
Awn i'r nant a phryf a bach,
ac yn iach i newyn;
odid fawr na chawn ni blwc
ac wrth lwc bysgodyn.'

St. David's Feast Day

Let everyone sing on St. David's day morning, all the children of earth. Everyone from Adam's line should have a smile on his face for this is the feast day of fishing!

David was weak during Lent, in the season of fasting. He suffered terribly through his nose—for Paradise sake!—for he would wake in the night, faint with hunger, after dreaming of roast pork.

But heaven heard his prayer and twenty trout appeared, dry from the river; and there was a pan on the fire singing for supper and there were the trout in a row spitting in the heat.

'Then let us eat' said Saint David, 'let us eat a hundred of them. Such a fine meal is no sin (i.e. one may eat fish during Lent). Let's to the stream with rod and line whenever we feel hungry; let's hope for a bite and, with any luck, a fish.'

Ar ol glaw nid oedai fyth
godi'n syth o'i gadair;
gwelid ef yn mynd i'w daith
ganwaith gyda genwair.
A'r angylion oll o'i blaid
nid oedd raid ymguddio;
nid oedd brithyll yn y dwr
nad oedd siwr ohono.

Iawn coffau'r hen Ddewi Sant
Draw wrth nant y mynydd,
gyda'r dorlan, gyda'r brwyn
dan y llwyn mewn llonydd;
ac wrth fynd drwy'r grug a'r llus
hapus fydd y canu,
yn nhawelwch mawr y rhos
gyda'r nos yn nesu.

John Glyn Davies, 1870-1953

Cywydd Dewi Sant

"Cystal om ardal imi,
Dwywaith vyned at Dewi,
A phe delwn cystlwn cain,
O riv unwai i Ruvain,
Myned dairgwaith araith yw
Am enaid, hyd y Mynyw
I mae'n cystal a myned,
I vedd Crist unwaith vydd cred.

Bedd Crist Cymmru ddidrist cain,
A ryvedd deml o Ruvain,
Dewi a bair gywir ged,
I' werin gymru wared,
Dewi ddyvrws yw'n diwyd,
Davydd ben saint bedydd byd,
O nev i daeth ffyrv goeth ffydd
I nev i ddaeth yn yvydd."

Ieuan ap Rhydderch. 15th cent.

So whenever it had been raining, he'd always get out of his chair and go off with his rod, oh a hundred times! And all the angels were on his side so he never needed to skulk in the bushes; there wasn't a trout in the river he couldn't catch.

It is good to remember dear Saint David near the mountain stream, on the bank amongst the rushes and under the bushes; and coming home through the heather and the bilberries, happily singing in the peace of the evening as the night draws in.

It is as good for me, from my area,
to go twice to Dewi,
As if I should go, fine relation,
One time to Rome.
To go three times, this is golden work,
For my soul's sake as far as Mynyw, (St. Davids)
It is as good as going
To Christ's grave once, the blessing of Christendom.
This is the Grave of Christ, in fair blessed Wales
And his remarkable temple, and his Rome.
Dewi will bring about, a ready gift,
Deliverance to the Welsh folk.
Dewi who drinks only water is our follower,
Dewi is the chief of all the world's baptized saints.
From heaven came strong and rich faith,
To heaven he returned obediently.

(Literal translation)

The following poem is taken from Gwynfardd Brycheiniog's ode of praise to Saint David and to the 'clas' (Monastic Community) at St. Davids. The Reverend Wyn Evans, an authority on St. Davids, disputes this connection and suggests rather that it is the sister church at Llanddewi Brefi which is lauded here. Indeed the extract taken here would seem to indicate the same, especially the references to the boundaries of David's cult—coinciding with the rivers in the vicinity of Llanddewi Brefi—not St. Davids.

The Power of David

Diogel ei nawdd i'r neb a'i cyrcho diogan ei fro diogyweg
Rhag creirea Dewi yd gryn Groeg
Ac Iwerddon dirion dir Gwyddeleg
O garawn gan jawn gan ehoeg
Hyd a Dyfi afon firain a theg
O'r Llyn ddu lled fu llid gyhydreg
Hyd ar Twrch terfyn tir a charreg
Doddyw i Ddewi yn heneg
Gan borth Duw porth dyn yn ddiatreg
Dothyw i Ddewi diffreidiad teg
Rhys mawr Mon wledig reodig reg.
Rhy meddyliais i hyn i hofni
Urddawl, ei urddas anfeidrawl a feddy roddi
Rhwyf radeu bieu beirdd i'w foli
A llen, a llyfreu, a llen bali.

Pan deuth o ffrainc ffrangc i oer erchi
Icchyd rhag clefyd rhag clwyf delli
Wynep-clawr didawr dim ni welai
Pesychwys, tremwys, trwy fodd Dewi
Merch brenhin dwyrain doeth i Frefi
A phryd a gweryd y gud a hi
Wrth glywed dahed tynghed Dewi
A'i fuchedd wirionedd wirion ynni

There is a latin inscription on a stone at Llanddewi Brefi Church—HIC IACET IDNERT FILIUS JACOBI QUI OCCISUS FUIT PROPTER PREDAM SANCTI DAVID, with the overall meaning: 'Here lies Idnerth, Son of Jacob, who was killed while defending the church of the Holy David from despoilation.'

I wonder whether this has any connection with the extract quoted? The poem was wrttien c. 1175-1200. The extract is from lines 140-165 from a poem of 295 lines.

There is not a great deal of spirituality in this extract. It is a typical 12th Century attempt to boost Saint David's cult—to stress his prime position in Wales and to oppose all attempts to make Saint Davids subserviant to the Archbishop of Canterbury.

His sanctuary is stedfast for all who seek it
His area is blameless, faultless.
Before Dewi's relics Greece itself would quake
And fair Ireland, land of the Irish.
From the (river) Caron by truth through purple heather,
Unto the Tywi, noble and fair river;
From Llyn ddu there was a stormy meeting,
As far as the Twrch boundary of land and stone.
There came adroitly unto Dewi
By God's support, by man's backing, without delay;
There came to Dewi a fair defender
Great Rhys, Lord of Anglesey, giver of generous gifts.

I thought to announce the noble one,
He can give of his infinite dignity;
He is the lord who has blessings—poets praise him,
And literature and books and satin cloth.
When there came from France a frenchman to ask of him,
A cure from a disease, blind from a malady,
An agitated flat-faced person who could see nothing,
He coughed, he could see through Dewi's will.
The daughter of an Eastern King came to Brefi,
And brought earth and soil with her;
Having heard how good was Dewi's destiny,
And his true life history, vigorous and innocent.

Awdl i Ddewi

D. Llwyd o Fathafarn, the poet, wrote in the second half of the 15th Century. Many of the references are obscure but it is generally believed that this particular ode was written shortly before the Battle of Bosworth and that he sought in it to enlist Saint David's support for Henry Tudor's cause.

Dewi, cyn d'eni caed ordeiniaw—man
mynyw i th weddiaw,
A Phadrig aeth i drigaw
O Fynyw dros yr hefn draw.

Dewi, lle'r wyd aed oll yr iaith,
Dyfod y mae rhyw adfyd maith,
Term anghyliaith, trwm, anghylion,

Dir i Gymru, rhag drwg amraint,
Draw dy foli, drud ofeilianint,
A gwylio'r naint, a galw ar Non.

Llawer gweddi rhag llwyr godded,
A blin oeddyn neb le nodded,
Dygn y'n rhodded, dwg nin rhyddion.

Y sawl sydd, a fu ac a fydd,
Pawb doed pob dydd i'n rhoi yn rhydd,
At bab y ffydd aed bawb a'i ffon.

Dyma'r amser y daw'r ymswrn
Y dewr yn ddig, a dur 'n eiddurn
Er enwi surn o'r ynys hon.

Llawer baner i'r llawr beunydd
Llawer gawr fawr yn floegra fydd
Lle mae brau gwydd llyma brig onn.

Dewi r ydym ar dy radau,
Bywyd eirwir ar baderau,
Y gwenerau, ac yn wirion

A'th weddiau dethau Ddewi,
Ruydd-dad, a wnaeth rydd-did inni,
I'th rieni, athro union.

Ode to Dewi

Dewi, before your birth a place was ordained,
Mynyw—for your praying
And Patrick went to live
From Mynyw over the hollow yonder.

Dewi, where you are, let all the nation go,
Some tedious affliction is coming,
An alien, heavy, unjust crisis.

It is necessary for Wales. In
case of an unfortunate loss of privilege,
To praise you yonder, grievous anxieties,

And to watch the streams, and to call upon Non.
Many prayers (were said)
(to keep us) from total pain,

And we were tired without a place of sanctuary.
We were placed grievously, we were led to be free.
Those who are, who have been, and who will be,

Let everyone come each day to set us free,
To the faith's Pope let everyone take his staff (support)
This is the time the turmoil will come
The brave (will be) angry, with steel in his fist,
Though a good number have been called from this island.

Many banners will bite the dust each day
There will be many loud cries in England,
Where there are withered trees,
there will be the topmost branches of the ash tree.

Dewi we are dependent on your blessings,
A sincere life, based on prayers
and fastings, and innocent.

And your own prayers Dewi,
Generous father, gave us freedom,
To your parents, true teacher.

Ac eleni disgwyl Wynedd
Y cawn weled can nialedd
Y gelanedd eur gelynion

Gelynion a drig eleni—ym maes
  Cyn diwedd mis Medi
pob tir maith, pawb o'n iaith ni
pob tuedd, pawb at Dewi.

Seren ddisglair nef yn twynnu,
Tyst diysgog cyfraith Iesu,
Hyn yw Dewi yn ein gwlad;
Pery yn ei santaidd fywyd,
Yn ei wir athrawiaeth hefyd,
Addurn pennaf Mynyw fad.

Fel yng ngeni y Bedyddiwr,
Caed am fywyd pur ein noddwr
Ragfynegiad dwyfol cudd;
Nodir mawredd gwas yr Arglwydd
Gan y nef drwy lawer arwydd:
Mêl a dwr a'r cyflym hydd.

Dyma arwr mawr ein brodir,
Llyw ac athro Cymry cywir,
Cynorthwywr teulu Ior;
Mwyn ei galon, rhwysg wrthododd
Ffodd o'r ddinas, encil fynnodd
Addas i grefyddol gor.

Enwyd ef yn 'Ddewi Ddyfrwr'
Fan y werin, fel dilynwr
Ympryd, dirwest, tra bu fyw;
Gwel y dall, diflanna heintiau,
Ffy y Fall trwy rinwedd geiriau
Salmydd cu Efengyl Duw.

And this year Gwynedd expects
That we shall see a hundred retributions
Our enemies—a heap of dead bodies
Enemies will die this year—in the field (of battle)
Before the end of September
Every distant land, everyone of our language (nation)
Every persuasion, everyone (will come) to Dewi.

The Medieval Sequence of Saint David

David, Star of heavenly splendour,
Latter Covenant's Defender,
Glitters o'er Britannia;
By his holy conversation,
By the true Faith's conversation,
He adorns Menevia.

As the Harbinger was named
By the Angel, so proclaimed
Was he e'er his natal day;
Hart and honey, water flowing,
Mystic signs of fame foreshowing,
Christ's devoted thrall portray.

He, the Britons' champion fearless,
Of the Welsh the teacher peerless,
Takes the heavenly freemen's part:
Now the Sage, the city quitting,
Seek the vale's retreat befitting
Men of humbleness of heart.

Dewi Sant his sons acclaim him!
From his birth the people name him
Dewi Ddyfrwr—'Waterman';
Halt and maimed and blind he healeth,
Satan in confusion reeleth
At the Christian Psalmist's ban.

Doeth yng nghyfraith lân y Drindod,
Lluniodd gyfrol fu'n rhyfeddod
I holl ddeiliaid Teyrnas Dduw;
Dewi dirion, arwr nerthol,
Trecha dithau drwy dy eiriol
Erchyll elyn dynol ryw.

Silfan

Early 15th Century Hereford Missal

Mair o Fynyw

There is a rare representation of Joachim and Anna, Mother of the Blessed Virgin Mary on the south side of the altar built up of very ancient stones in the Holy Trinity Chapel in St. David's Cathedral. The following poem from the anthology of the poems of Hywel Swrdwal by J. C. Morrice has great affinity of spirit to Mary and the shrine of David.

I Sioassym ac i Anna Mam Mair

Am ddeuddyn ymddyweddi
sy'n y nef (y) soniwn ni . . .

Ni chaed merch iechyd ymyw
mor, feinael Mair o fynyw
maer Kor wrth yr ystoria
yno yn wir ag iawn a wna
mae i thad, ni ad un yn nes
mae Anna yn i mynwes
mae Mair yn un air a ni
mae plaid mendwyaid Dewi
mae siartr mab duw gartref
mae Sioseb yn wneb nef
mae'r mab rhad yn yr aberth
mae Mair yn un air ai nerth.

Hywel Swrdwal 1430-1460

Whilst a treatise he was writing,
God, this man of law requiting,
Gilds the letters of the tome;
Holy David, be our Pleader,
As thy namesake, be our Leader,
Our Goliath overcome!

trans. Athelstan Riley

Of two betrothed people
who are in heaven, we shall talk . . .

No girl alive and well can be found
as fine browed as Mary of Mynyw (St. Davids)
The choir, according to the history
Is there, indeed, and it will make amends.
Her father is there, no one is nearer.
Anna is in her heart.
Mair is of one voice with us.
There is a society of Dewi's hermits.
The Son of God's charter is on earth.
Joseph is in heaven's honour.
The blessed son is in the Mass.
Mair is of one voice with her host.

(Literal Translation)

From *The Hymn to the Virgin*

O michti ladi, owr leding/tw haf
at hefn owr abeiding:
yntw ddy ffest efrlesting
i set a braents ws tw bring.

I wann ddys wyth blys, ddy blesing/off God
ffor iwr gwd abering,
hwier i bynn ffor iwr wyning
syns kwin, and iwr swnn ys king.

Owr ffadyrs ffadyr, owr ffiding,/owr pop,
on iwr paps had swking;
yn hefn-blys i haf thys thing,
atendans wythowt ending.

Wi sin ddy bricht kwin wyth kwning/and blys,
ddy bloswm ffruwt bering;
ei wowld, as owld as ei sing,
wynn iwr lwf on iwr lofing.

Kwin od off owr God, owr geiding/mwdyr,
maedyn notsythstanding,
hwo wed syts wyth a ryts ring
as God wod ddys gwd weding.

Help ws, prae ffor ws, preffering/owr sowls;
Asoel ws at owr ending.
Mak ddat awl wi ffawl tw ffing
iwr swns lwf, owr syns lefing.

As wi mae ddy dae off deiing/resef
owr safiowr yn howsling;
as hi mae tak ws waking
tw wwn yn hys michti wing.

O mighty lady, our leading/to have
at heaven our abiding:
to bring us unto the everlasting feast
ye planted a branch (=of Jesse's tree)

Ye won this with bliss, the blessing/of God
for your good child-bearing,
where ye are for your reward
since queen, and your Son is king.

Our father's father, our feeding,/our pope,
was nourished at your breast;
in heaven's bliss ye have this thing (namely)
service without ending.

We see the bright queen with wisdom/and bliss,
the blossom bearing fruit;
I would for as long as I sing
win your love in praising you.

Sole queen of our God, our guiding/mother,
maiden notwithstanding,
who wed such with a rich ring
since God desired this good wedding.

Help us, pray for us, favouring/our souls;
Absolve us at our ending.
Grant that we all consent to accept
your Son's love, our sins leaving.

So that we may the day of dying/receive
our saviour in communion;
that he may take us wakeful
to dwell in his mighty wing.

Michti, i twk, mi ocht tw tel
owt, sowls off hel tw soels off hicht.
Wi aes wyth bwk, wi wys wyth bel,
tw hefn ffwl wel tw haf on fflicht
  awl dids wel dwn,
  tabeit te bwn—
  a god-mat trwn,
    a gwd, mit wricht;
  and si so swn
  and north and nwn
  an swnn an mwn
    an swnn on micht.

* * *

O trysti Kreist tat werst a krown,
er wi dei down, aredi dicht,
  tw thank tw thi
  at te rwt-tri.
  Dden went awl wi,
    ddein own, tw light.
  Tw grawnt agri,
  amen, wy mi,
  ddat ei mae si
    ddi tw mei sicht!

Owr lwk, owr king, owr lok, owr kae—
mei God, ei prae, mei geid wpricht!
Ei sik, ei sing, ei siak, ei sae,
ei wer awae, a wiri wicht.
  Agast ei go,
  mei ffrynds mi ffro.
  Ei ffond a ffo,
    wy ffynd ei fficht;
  eil sing awlso
  yn welth an wo
  (ei kann no mo)
    tw kwin o micht.

Ieuan Ap Hywel Swrdwal
(fl. 1430-1480)

Mighty, he took (I must tell it
out) souls from hell to regions on high.
We ask with book, we wish with bell,
to heaven full well to have in flight
all well-done deeds,
to abide the reward—
a throne made by God,
a good, true craftsman;
and see thus soon
both north and noon
and sun and moon
and the Son in might.

* * *

O trusty Christ that wearest a crown,
ere we die down, already dressed
to give thee thanks
at the rood-tree.
Then wend all we,
thine own, to light.
To grant agree,
amen, with me,
that I may see
thee to my sight!

Our luck, our kind, our lock, our key—
my God, I pray, my upright guide!
I seek, I sing, I shake, I speak,
I wear away, a weary wight.
Aghast I go,
far from my friends.
I find a foe,
with fiend I fight;
I'll sing also
in wealth and woe
(I can do no more)
to the queen of might.

(A literal version)

Swper yr Arglwydd

'Roedd haint yn yr awyr a golwg go sâl ar bethau,
A holl liwiau natur ag ymyl o inclyd ystaen,
A bugail ar ochr bryn yn crynhoi 'i ddefaid a'u cyfri,
Cyfri defaid twp o bechodau pryfedig a braen.

'Roedd hi'n dawel yn yr Eglwys, ac yn y tawelwch ddychryn,
Dychryn rhag yr allor a'r Groes a'r dwyrain yn y gwydr,
A'r gangell mor ddieithr o bell a'r nen uwch ei phen mor uchel,
A ni yn y pant yn penlinio fel tyweirch tywyll a budr.

Daeth Bethlem i lawr o'r nef i ganol gwasanaeth y Cymun,
Gyda'i hangylion a'i bugeiliaid a'i hanifeiliaid anfodlon fud,
A Mair yn clymu'n dwt anfeidroldeb Duw yn ei gewyn,
Ac yn siglo tragwyddoldeb i gysgu yn ei grud.

Ni luchiodd ein tipyn cnawd fel cerpyn ar domennydd Gehenna,
Na thaflu yno ein gwaed fel potel o foddion gwyw,
Ond eu codi o afael tridiau digyffelyb y pryfed
Yn gorff ysbrydol dryloyw perffeithrwydd dyn a Duw.

'Roedd swn disgyn dwr yn y gangell fel ar sgwar dinas yn yr Eidal,
Gofer ar hyd gwely defod a defosiwn o ffynhonnau'r nef
A phelydryn yn chwarae o amgylch y groes gan bylu'r ddwy gannwyll,
Pelydryn o goelcerth Ei ddynoliaeth ddwyfol Ef.

A thu allan troes duwch marwol yr yw yn Llanbadarn
Yn wanwyn o wyrdd a hwnnw yn orlawn o gân,
A'r mor yn carlamu i gofleidio Rheidol ac Ystwyth
A'i ewyn yn fflam a'i donnau i gyd ar dân.

Gwenallt

(The poet was accustomed to worship in the ancient church at Llanbadarn Fawr, Aberystwyth)

The Lord's Supper

There was disease in the air and things had an ill appearance,
All nature's colours were edged with an inky stain,
A shepherd on a hillside gathered his sheep and counted them,
Counted the sheep stupid with wormeaten rotten sins.

It was quiet in the Church, and in the quietness fright,
Horror of the altar and the Cross and the east in the glass,
And the chancel so far unfamiliar and the roof over its head so high
And us down on the low ground kneeling like dark and dirty clods.

Bethlehem came down from heaven into the middle of the communion service,
With its angels and shepherds and its mute, discontented animals,
And Mary tidily folding up God's immortality in her sinews,
And rocking eternity in his cradle to sleep.

He did not fling our bit of flesh like a rag on the rubbish-dumps of Gehenna,
Or throw our blood there like a bottle of worn-out medicine,
But raised them from the grip of the worms' incomparable three days
A transparent spiritual body, the perfection of man and God.

There was a sound of trickling water in the chancel like in the square of an Italian city,
A streamlet along the bed of ritual and worship from the wells of heaven,
And a sunbeam playing around the cross obliterating the light of two candles,
A spark from the bonfire of His divine humanity.

And outside, the deadly darkness of the yew tree in Llanbadarn
Became a green spring bursting all over with song,
And the sea galloped in to embrace Rheidol and Ystwyth,
And its foam was aflame and all its waves were on fire.

Cywydd i Ferch o Fôn oedd myned i Offrwm i Fynyw, am ladd y bardd a'i thraserch

Gwawr ddyhuddiant y cantref
Lleiau aeth er llu o nef,
Ac er Non, calon a'i cel,
Ac er Dewi, eigr dawel;
O Fon deg, boed rhwydd rhegddi
I Fynyw dir, f'enaid i!
I geisiaw blodeuaw'r blaid,
Maddeuant am a ddywaid,
Am ladd ei gwas dulas dig,
Penydiwr cul poenedig;
O alanas gwas gwawdferw,
Yr aeth oer hiraeth ar herw;
Greddf ffoes gruddiau ffuon,
Gadewis fy newis Fon.
Crist arglwydd! boed rhwydd y trae
Cas, a chymynas Menai;
Y Traeth Mawr, goludfawr glod,
Treia, gad fyned trwod.
Y Bychan Draeth, gaeth gerynt,
Gad im'dyn gwyn hyn o hynt;
Darfu'r gweddiau dirfawr,
Digyffro fo Ertro fawr!
Talwnfferm porth Abermaw
Ar don drae, er ei dwyn draw;
Gydne gwin, gad naw gwaneg,
Dysyni i dir Dewi deg;
A dwfn yw tonau Dyfi,
Dwfr rhyn, yn ei herbyn hi;
Theidiol, gad er d'anrhydedd,
Heol i fun hael o fedd;
Ystwyth, ymhwyth, gad im'hon,
Drais dew-ddwfr; dros dy ddwyfron;
Aeron, ferw hyson hoywserch,
Gad trwod fy eurglod ferch;
Teifi, dw'r tyfiad eurwawn,
Gad i'r dyn gadeirio dawn;

A day of promise dawns for the whole neighbourhood: Morfudd the Nun (my dear love) is going from Mona on her pilgrimage to Mynyw to seek forgiveness through the heavenly hosts, through St. Non and Saint David for the words that killed her angry lover. A thin tormented penitent she seeks forgiveness with offerings of flowers from the guilt of this young man whose boiling song is dead; so now she goes in grief and longing on her journey. Morfudd's heart is secret, her lips silent: let this journey be safe and easy for her.

When you leave my lovely isle of Mona it is as if the colour drained from ruddy cheeks; Lord Jesus let her have an easy crossing! Kind straits of Menai let her through, Traeth Mawr beach let your tide ebb and let her pass. Traeth-Mawr and Traeth-Bach you estuaries joined like lovers, let my dear pass on her journey. I can make no greater prayer than this, be calm for her, great Arthro; I would give the price of a farm for an ebb wave to carry her across the estuary at Barmouth.

And now deep Dovey with your wine-dark flood and shivering waters, let nine waves carry her to sweet St. David's country. Rheidiol for your honour's sake give passage to her: Ystwyth grant this to me, a crossing of fair water between your two banks. Boiling Aeron, noisy and nimble like a lover, let through my golden love. Teifi, springing golden water, let her pass beyond your spreading grace,

Durfing drwy'r afon derfyn,
Yr el ac y del y dyn.
Mam hirffawd, mae ymhorffor,
Os byw, rhwng Mynyw a'r mor;
Os hi a'm lladdodd, oes hir;
Herw hylithr, hwyr yr holir,
Maddeued Mair, neddair nawdd,
I'm lleddf wylan a'm lladdawdd,
Diau mae im a'i dihaur,
Minau a'i maddau i'm haur.

Dafydd ap Gwilym

Lo, between the myrtles standing,
One who merits well my love,
Though His worth I guess but dimly,
High all earthly things above;
Happy morning
When at last I see him clear!

Rose of Sharon, so men name Him;
White and red His cheeks adorn;
Store untold of earthly treasure
Will His merit put to scorn;
Friend of sinners,
He their pilot o'er the deep.

What can weigh with me henceforward
All the idols of the earth?
One and all I here proclaim them,
Match with Jesus, nothing worth;
O to rest me
All my lifetime in His love!

Ann Griffiths (1776-1805)
translated from the Welsh by Sir Idris Bell

carry her strongly to the river's mouth, so let her come to the end of her journey.

Holy Mother of all happiness robed in purple, who lives between Mynyw and the sea, though my love has killed me, let her long escape, and let it be long till she is called to reckoning. May Mary with her hand of charity, forgive my gentle seabird who has killed me. Though I am the one who should defend myself, freely I forgive her for the harm she did me.

Translation by Nigel Heseltine

From *The Spiritual Canticle*

My Beloved is the mountains,
The wooded valleys, lonely and sequestered,
The strange and distant islands,
The loud resounding rivers,
The loving breezes with their gentle whispers.

The still and tranquil night
As it kindles with the coming dawn,
The music that is silent,
The ringing solitude,
The supper that refreshes and awakens love.

St. John of the Cross

I am the sounding wave
my hand is the voice of the sea.
It swims with the seal in his laughter.
The sacrament of being
you share with me.

Ray Howard Jones

Cymru—Wales

The dust of all the saints of the ages
And the martyrs lies in your bosom;
It was you who gave them breath,
And you who took it from them.

The angels would be walking here,
Their footprints on your roadways,
And the Holy Spirit nested
Dovelike in your branches.

Poets heard on wind and breeze
His cry of sacrifice, His gasp of pain,
And in the middle of your forests
The Tree of the Cross was seen.

His resurrection was your springtide,
Your summer was His green salvation,
And in the winter of your mountains
He raised tabernacles of grace.

The dew and rain of Providence He shed
On your cornfields and your oats,
And His glory was on the trappings
And the bridles of your chargers.

Your boats and your sailing-ships
Glided over the seaways,
With merchandise of Calvary
Stowed beneath their deckboards.

God chose you for his handmaiden,
And called on your for witness;
And He inscribed His Covenant
On your doors and your doorposts.

Your saints are a noble fellowship,
They love you, and you love them,
And you gather them under your wing
Like chicks in under the hen.

Gwenallt

The Woodland Mass

A pleasant place I was at today,
under mantles of the worthy green hazel,
listening at day's beginning
to the skilful cock thrush
singing a splendid stanza
of fluent signs and symbols;
a stranger here, wisdom his nature,
a brown messenger who had journeyed far,
coming from rich Carmarthenshire
at my golden girl's command.
About him was a setting
of flowers of the sweet boughs of May,
like green mantles, his chasuble
was of the wings of the wind.
There was here, by the great God,
nothing but gold in the altar's canopy.
I heard, in polished language,
a long and faultless chanting,
an unhesitant reading to the people
of a gospel without mumbling;
the elevation, on the hill for us there,
of a good leaf for a holy wafer.
Then the slim eloquent nightingale
from the corner of a grove nearby,
poetess of the valley, sings to the many
the Sanctus bell in lively whistling.
The sacrifice is raised
up to the sky above the bush,
devotion to God the Father,
the chalice of ecstasy and love.
The psalmody contents me;
it was bred of a birch-grove in the sweet woods.

Dafydd ap Gwilym

Psalm to the Creatures

Let us celebrate the single-cloaked beings
Content in their coats of fur and feathers,
And the swimmers who wish to other garb than their
  skins.

Let us sing
The ants who do not reckon their hours of diligence
  on their hillock-years
Because a forest of heather-bells
Sweetens their labour;
The common newt who is wiser than men,
And the woolly-bear who zig-zags on cabbage wine.

Let us envy
The cormorant who bathes in the precious colours
Of sunset on the sea;
The salmon, sunny his bliss,
Who knows how to breed young without charity;
The moon—drunk owl
Proud because night is the other side of day,
And the squirrel who slinks to Annwfn
To doze away the long barren season.

Let us weave praise
For the birds of legends,
Noah's dove and Brasswen's starling
Who carried the mail across the waters.
And Rhiannon's birds
Who gave merry nights to the dead
And caused bones to dance.

And let us not forget
The hopping gander
Who gave a few quills to Bishop Morgan,
Giving the haven of its wings to the Welsh language,
And the mother-hens who provided
Welsh beds with their warmth.

Gwilym R. Jones: Salm i'r Creaduriaid

The Creatures

Let the heavens and the earth praise Him, the Glorious, and every creature which is in heaven and on earth and under the earth, in the seas and all that are in them.
Let us praise and exalt Him above all forever.

Writings of Saint Francis

The Canticle

O most high, almighty, good Lord God, to Thee belong praise, glory, honour, and all blessing!
Praised be my Lord God with all His creatures; and specially our brother the sun who brings us the day, and who brings us the light; fair is he, and shining with a very great splendour: O Lord, to us he signifies Thee!
Praised be my Lord for our sister the moon, and for the stars, the which He has set clear and lovely in heaven.
Praised be my Lord for our brother the wind, and for air and cloud, calms and all weather, by the which Thou upholdest in life all creatures.
Praised be my Lord for our sister water, who is very serviceable unto us, and humble, and precious, and clean.
Praised be my Lord for our brother fire, through whom Thou givest us light in the darkness; and he is bright, and pleasant, and very mighty, and strong.
Praised be my Lord for our mother the earth, the which doth sustain and keep us, and bringeth forth divers fruits, and flowers of many colours, and grass.
Praised be my Lord for all those who pardon one another for His love's sake, and who endure weakness and tribulation; blessed are they who peaceably shall endure, for Thou, O Most Highest, shalt give them a crown.
Praised be my Lord for our sister, the death of the body, from whom no man escapeth. Woe to him who dieth in mortal sin!
Blessed are they who are found walking by Thy most holy will, for the second death shall have no power to do them harm.
Praise ye, and bless ye the Lord, and give thanks unto Him, and serve Him with great humility.

St. Francis

Scribes Reverie

A hedge of trees surrounds me,
A blackbird's lay sings to me;
Above my lines booklet
The trilling birds chant to me.

In a grey mantle from the top of bushes
The cuckoo sings;
Verily—may the Lord shield me—
Well do I write under the greenwood.
Early ninth century Irish Poem.

Celtic Idyll

I wish, O Son of the living God, O ancient, eternal King,
For a hidden little hut in the wilderness that it may be my dwelling.
An all-grey lithe little lark to be by its side,
A clear pool to wash away sins through the grace of the Holy Spirit . . .
A southern aspect for warmth, a little brook across its floor,
A choice land with many gracious gifts such as be good for every plant . . .
A pleasant church and with the linen altar-cloth, a dwelling for God from Heaven;
Then, shining candles above the pure white Scriptures . . .
This is the husbandry I would take, I would choose, and will not hide it:
Fragrant leek, hens, salmon, trout, bees.
Raiment and food enough for me from the King of fair fame,
And I to be sitting for a while praying to God in every place.
Seventh Century Irish Poem.

Late Have I Loved You

Late have I loved You
O beauty ever ancient, ever new!
Late have I loved You
And behold,
You were within; and I without,
and without I sought You.
And deformed I ran after these forms
of beauty You have made.
You were with me
And I was not with You.
Those things held me back from You,
things whose only being
was to be in You.
You called; You cried;
and You broke through my deafness.
You flashed; You shone;
and You chased away my blindness.
You became fragrant;
and I inhaled and sighed for You.
I tasted and now hunger and thirst for You.
You touched me;
and I burned for Your embrace.

Prayer of St. Augustine

I gaze across the distant hills,
Thy coming to espy;
Beloved, haste, the day grows late,
The sun sinks down the sky.

All the old loves I followed once
Are now unfaithful found;
But a sweet sickness holds me yet
Of love that has no bound!

Love that the sensual heart ne'er knows,
Such power, such grace it brings,
Which sucks desire and thought away
From all created things.

O make me faithful while I live,
Attuned to thy praise,
And may no pleasure born of earth
Entice to devious ways.

All my affections now withdraw
From objects false, impure,
To the one object which unchanged
Shall to the last endure.

There is no station under heaven
Where I have lust to live;
Only the mansions of God's house
Can perfect pleasure give.

Regard is dead and lust is dead
For the world's gilded toys;
Her ways are nought but barrenness,
And vain are all her joys.

William Williams of Pantycelyn (1716-91)
translated from the Welsh by Sir Idris Bell

Guide me, O thou great Jehovah,
Pilgrim through this barren land;
I am weak, but Thou art mighty;
Hold me with Thy powerful hand:
Bread of heaven,
Feed me now and evermore.

Open now the crystal fountain,
Whence the healing stream doth flow;
Let the fiery cloudy pillar
Lead me all my journey through:
Strong Deliverer,
Be Thou still my strength and shield.

When I tread the verge of Jordan,
Bid my anxious fears subside;
Death of death, and hell's Destruction,
Land me safe on Canaan's side.
Songs of praises
I will ever give to Thee.

William Williams of Pantycelyn

O'er those gloomy hills of darkness
Look, my soul; be still, and gaze;
All the promises do travail
With a glorious day of grace:
Blessed Jubil
Let thy glorious morning dawn.

Kingdoms wide that sit in darkness,
Let them have the glorious light;
And from eastern coast to western
May the morning chase the night,
And redemption,
Freely purchased win the day.

Lord, I long to see that morning,
When Thy Gospel shall abound,
And Thy grace get full possession
Of the happy promised ground;
All the borders
Of the great Immanuel's land.

Fly aboard, eternal gospel,
Win and conquer, never cease;
May thy lasting wide dominions
Multiply and still increase;
May thy sceptre
Sway the enlightened world around.

William Williams of Pantycelyn

David of the White Rock

Give me my harp, my companion so long,
Let it once more add its voice to my song,
Tho' my old fingers are palsied and weak
Still my good harp for its master will speak.

Often the hearts of our chiefs it has stirred,
When its loud summons to battle was heard;
Harp of my country, dear harp of the brave,
Let thy last notes linger over my grave.

Translated by John Oxenford

Thanksgiving

Thanks to Thee, O God, that I have risen today,
To the rising of this life itself;
May it be to Thine own glory, O God of every gift,
And to the glory of my soul likewise.

O Great God, aid Thou my soul
With the aiding of Thine own mercy;
Even as I clothe my body with wool,
Cover Thou my soul with the shadow of Thy wing.

Help me to avoid every sin,
And the source of every sin to forsake;
And as the mist scatters on the crest of the hills,
May each ill haze clear from my soul, O God.

Irish Prayer for Light and Guidance

Be thou my vision, O Lord of my heart,
Be all else but naught to me, save that thou art;
Be thou my best thought in the day and the night,
Both walking and sleeping, thy presence my light.
Be thou my wisdom, be thou my true word,
Be thou ever with me, and I with thee Lord;
Be thou my great Father, and I thy true son;
Be thou in me dwelling, and I with thee one.
Be thou my breastplate, my sword for the fight;
Be thou my whole armour, be thou my true might;
Be thou my soul's shelter, be thou my strong tower;
O raise thou me heavenward, great power of my power.
Riches I heed not, nor man's empty praise;
Be thou mine inheritance now and always;
Be thou and thou only the first in my heart:
O sovereign of heaven, my treasure thou art.
High king of heaven, thou heaven's bright sun
O grant me its joys after victory is won;
Great heart of my own heart, whatever befall,
Still be thou my vision, O ruler of all.

Morning Prayer

I belive, O God of all gods,
That Thou are the eternal Father of life;
I believe, O God of all gods,
That Thou art the eternal Father of love.

I believe, O God of all gods,
That Thou art the eternal Father of the saints;
I believe, O God of all gods,
That Thou art the eternal Father of each one.

I believe, O God of all gods,
That Thou are the eternal Father of mankind;
I believe, O God of all gods,
That Thou art the eternal Father of the world.

I believe, O Lord and God of the peoples,
That Thou art the creator of the high heavens,
That Thou art the creator of the skies above,
That Thou art the creator of the oceans below.

I believe, O Lord and God of the peoples,
That Thou art He Who created my soul and set its warp,
Who created my body from dust and from ashes,
Who gave to my body breath, and to my soul its possession.

Father, bless to me my body,
Father, bless to me my soul,
Father, bless to me my life,
Father, bless to me my belief.

Father eternal and Lord of the peoples,
I believe that Thou hast remedied my soul in the Spirit of healing,
That Thou gavest Thy loved Son in covenant for me,
That Thou has purchased my soul with the precious blood of Thy Son.
Father eternal and Lord of life,
I believe that Thou didst pour on me the Spirit of grace at the bestowal of baptism.

Prayer for going on a Journey

Bless to me, O God,
the earth beneath
my foot,
Bless to me, O God,
the path whereon
I go;
Bless to me, O God,
the thing of
my desire,

Thou evermore of evermore,
Bless Thou to me
my rest.

Bless to me the thing
whereon is set
my mind,
Bless to me the thing
whereon is set
my hope;

O Thou King of Kings,
Bless thou to me
mine eye.

O Holy
God of truth

O Loving
God of mercy,

sign me from the spells
sign me from the charms,
Compassionate
God of life;

forgiveness to me give,
In my wanton talk,
In my lying oath,
In my foolish deed,
In my empty speech.

As thou wast before
at my life's
beginning

Be thou so again
at my journey's
end.

As thou wast besides
at my soul's
shaping,

Father, be thou, too
at my journey's
close,

Be with me at each time,
Lying down
and arising,

Be with me in sleep
Companioned by
dear ones.

Thou,
my soul's healer,
keep me at even,
keep me at morning,
keep me at noon,

On rough course faring,
help and safeguard
my means this night.

I am tired,
astray,
and stumbling,

Shield thou me from
snare and sin.

My Christ!

My Christ!
my shield,
my encircler,
each day, each night,
each light,
each dusk.

My Christ!

My Christ!
my shield,
my encircler,
each day,
each night,
Each light, each dark.

Be near me,
uphold me,
My treasure,
my triumph.

Jesu,
Son of Mary!
my helper,
my encircler,
Jesu, Son of David!
my strength everlasting,
Jesu,
Son of Mary!
my helper,
my encircler,
Jesu,
Son of David!
my strength everlasting.

from Alexander Donald,
crofter, Borve, Barra.

The Pilgrim's Rune

King of the Elements—Love-father of Bliss,
In my pilgrimage from airt to airt,
From airt to airt,
May each evil be a good to me,
May each sorrow be a gladness to me,
And may Thy Son be my foster-brother,
Oh may Thy Son be my foster-brother.

Holy Spirit—Spirit of Light,
A pilgrim I throughout the night,
Throughout the night,
Lave my heart pure as the stars,
Lave my heart pure as the stars,
Nor fear I then the spells of evil,
The spells of evil.

Jesu—Son of the Virgin pure,
Be thou my pilgrim-staff throughout the lands,
Throughout the lands,
Thy love in all my thoughts, Thy likeness in my face,
May I heart-warm to others, and they heart-warm to me,
For love of the love of Thee,
For love of the love of Thee.

Celtic Rune of Hospitality

I saw a stranger yestreen,
I put food in the eating place,
drink in the drinking place,
music in the listening place,
and in the sacred name of the Triune
He blessed myself and my house,
my cattle and my dear ones,
and the lark said in her song
often, often, often,
goes the Christ in the stranger's guise.

No one of this nation ever begs, for the houses of all are common to all; and they consider liberality and hospitality amongst the first virtues.

Giraldus Cambrensis

Blessing of the Road

May the hills lie low,
May the sloughs fill up
In thy way.
May all evil sleep,
May all good awake,
In thy way.

Celtic Prayer

The Gospel of the God of Life
to shelter thee, to aid thee,
yea, the Gospel of Beloved Christ.
The holy Gospel of the Lord;
to keep from all malice,
from every dole and dolour;
to keep thee from all spite,
from evil eye and anguish.

Thou shalt travel thither,
thou shalt travel hither,
thou shalt travel
hill and headland,
thou shalt travel down,
thou shalt travel up,
thou shalt travel
ocean and narrow.

Christ Himself
is shepherd over thee,
enfolding thee on every side;
he will not
forsake thee
hand or foot,
nor let evil come
anigh thee.

Pilgrim's Rest

In Thy name O Jesu
who wast crucified
I lie down to rest;

watch Thou me
in sleep remote,
hold thou me
in Thy one hand;

watch Thou me
in sleep remote,
hold Thou me
in Thy one hand.

Bless me, O my Christ,
be thou my shield
protecting me,

aid my steps in
the pitiful swamp,
lead thou me
to the life eternal;

aid my steps
in the pitiful swamp,
lead thou me
to the life eternal.

Bless to me, O God,
the moon that is above me,
bless to me, O God,
the earth that is beneath me,

bless to me, O God,
my wife and my children,
and bless, O God,
myself who have care of them.

Bless to me
my wife and my
children,

and bless, O God,
myself
who have care
of them

Bless, O God, the thing
on which
mine eye doth rest.

Bless, O God, the thing
on which
my hope doth rest.

Bless, O God, my reason
and
my purpose.

Bless, O bless thou them,
Thou
God of Life;

Bless, O God
my reason and my purpose,

Bless, O Bless
Thou them,
Thou God of Life.

Celtic Prayer

Evening Prayer

Father eternal and Lord of mankind,
Enwrap Thou my body and my soul beloved,
Safeguard me this night in the sanctuary of Thy love,
Shelter me this night in the shelter of the saints.

Thou hast brought me up from last night
To the gracious light of this day,
Great joy to provide for my soul,
And to do excelling good to me.

Thanks be to Thee, Jesu Christ,
For the many gifts Thou hast bestowed on me,
Each day and night, each sea and land,
Each weather fair, each calm, each wild.

I am giving Thee worship with my whole life.
I am giving Thee assent with my whole power,
I am giving Thee praise with my whole tongue,
I am giving Thee honour with my whole utterance.

I am giving Thee reverence with my whole understanding,
I am giving Thee offering with my whole thought,
I am giving Thee praise with my whole fervour,
I am giving Thee humility in the blood of the Lamb.

I am giving Thee love with my whole devotion,
I am giving Thee kneeling with my whole desire,
I am giving Thee love with my whole heart,
I am giving Thee affection with my whole sense;
I am giving Thee my existence with my whole mind,
I am giving Thee my soul, O God of all gods.

My thought, my deed,
My word, my will,
My understanding, my intellect,
My way, my state.

I am beseeching Thee
To keep me from ill,
To keep me from hurt,
To keep me from harm;
To keep me from mischance,
To keep me from grief,
To keep me this night
In the nearness of Thy love.

May God shield me,
May God fill me,
May God keep me,
May God watch me.

May God bring me
To the land of peace,
To the country of the King,
To the peace of eternity.

Praise to the Father,
Praise to the Son,
Praise to the Spirit,
The Three in One.

The Sleep Prayer

I am now going into the sleep,
Be it that I in health shall waken;
If death be to me in the death-sleep,
Be it that on Thine own arm,
O God of Grace, I in peace shall waken;
  Be it on Thine own beloved arm,
  O God of Grace, that I in peace shall waken.

Be my soul on Thy right hand, O God,
Thou King of the heaven of heavens;
Thou it was who bought'st me with Thy blood,
Thou it was who gavest Thy life for me,
Encompass Thou me this night, O God,
That no harm, no evil shall me befall.

Whilst the body is dwelling in the sleep,
The soul is soaring in the shadow of heaven,
Be the red-white Michael meeting the soul,
Early and late, night and day,
Early and late, night and day.

The Guardian Angel

Thou angel of God who hast charge of me
From the dear Father of mercifulness,
The shepherding kind of the fold of the saints
To make round about me this night;

Drive from me every temptation and danger,
Surround me on the sea of unrighteousness,
And in the narrows, crooks, and straits,
Keep thou my coracle, keep it always.

Be thou a bright flame before me,
Be thou a guiding star above,
Be thou a smooth path below me,
And be a kindly shepherd behind me,
Today, tonight, and for ever.

I am tired and I a stranger,
Lead thou me to the land of angels;
For me it is time to go home
To the court of Christ, to the peace of heaven.

The Invocation of the Graces

I bathe thy palms
In showers of wine,
In the lustral fire,
In the seven elements,
In the juice of the rasps,
In the milk of the honey,
And I place the nine pure choice graces
In thy fair fond face,
    The grace of form,
    The grace of voice,
    The grace of fortune,
    The grace of goodness,
    The grace of charity,
    The grace of choice maidenliness,
    The grace of whole-souled loveliness,
    The grace of goodly speech.

Dark is the yonder town,
Dark are those therein,
Thou art the brown swan,
Going in among them.
Their hearts are under thy control,
Their tongues are beneath thy sole,
Nor will they ever utter a word
    To give thee offence.

A shade art thou in the heat,
A shelter art thou in the cold,
Eyes art thou to the blind,
A staff art thou to the pilgrim,
An island art thou at sea,
A fortress art thou on land,
A well art thou in the desert,
    Health art thou to the ailing.

Thine is the skill of the Fairy Woman,
Thine is the virtue of Bride the calm,
Thine is the faith of Mary the mild,
Thine is the tact of the woman of Greece,
Thine is the beauty of Emir the lovely,
Thine is the tenderness of Darthula delightful,
Thine is the courage of Maebh the strong,
    Thine is the charm of Binne-bheul.

Thou art the joy of all joyous things,
Thou art the light of the beam of the sun,
Thou art the door of the chief of hospitality,
Thou art the surpassing star of guidance,
Thou art the step of the deer of the hill,
Thou art the step of the steed of the plain,
Thou art the grace of the swan of swimming,
    Thou art the loveliness of all lovely desires.

The lovely likeness of the Lord,
Is in thy pure face,
The loveliest likeness that
Was upon earth.

The best hour of the day be thine,
The best day of the week be thine,
The best week of the year be thine,
The best year in the Son of God's domain be thine.

Peter has come and Paul has come,
James has come and John has come,
Muriel and Mary Virgin have come,
Uriel the all-beneficient has come,
Ariel the beauteousness of the young has come,
Gabriel the seer of the Virgin has come,
Raphael the prince of the valiant has come,
And Michael the chief of the hosts has come,
    And Jesus Christ the mild has come,
    And the Spirit of true guidance has come,
    And the King of kings has come on the helm,
    To bestow on thee their affection and their love,
      To bestow on thee their affection and their love.

The Guiding Light of Eternity

O God, who brought me from the rest of last night
unto the joyous light of this day,
Be Thou bringing me from the new light of this day
Unto the guiding light of eternity.
    Oh! from the new light of this day
    Unto the guiding light of eternity.

The Baptism Blessing

Thou Being who inhabitest the heights
Imprint Thy blessing betimes,
Remember Thou the child of my body,
In Name of the Father of peace;
When the priest of the King
On him puts the water of meaning,
Grant him the blessing of the Three
    Who fill the heights.
  The blessing of the Three
    Who fill the heights.

Sprinkle down upon him Thy grace,
Give Thou to him virtue and growth,
Give Thou to him strength and guidance,
Give Thou to him flocks and possessions,
Sense and reason void of guile,
Angel wisdom in his day,
That he may stand without reproach
    In Thy presence.
  He may stand without reproach
    In Thy presence.

Good Wish

Power of raven be thine,
Power of eagle be thine,
    Power of the Son.

Power of storm be thine,
Power of moon be thine,
    Power of heaven.

Goodness of sea be thine,
Goodness of earth be thine,
    Goodness of heaven.

Each day be joyous to thee,
No day be grievous to thee,
    Honour and compassion.

Love of each face be thine,
Death on pillow be thine,
    Thy Saviour's presence.

Peace

Peace between neighbours,
Peace between kindred,
Peace between lovers,
In love of the King of life.

Peace between person and person,
Peace between wife and husband,
Peace between woman and children,
The peace of Christ above all peace.

Bless, O Christ, my face,
Let my face bless every thing;
Bless, O Christ, mine eye,
Let mine eye bless all it sees.

Joyous Death

Give Thou to me, O God,
Each food that is needful for my body;
Give Thou to me, O God,
Each light that is needful for my mind;
Give Thou to me, O God
Each salve that is needful for my soul.

Give Thou to me, O God,
Sincere repentance;
Give Thou to me, O God,
Whole-hearted repentance;
Give Thou to me, O God,
Lasting repentance.

Give Thou to me, O God,
The death of the priceless oil;
Give Thou to me, O God,
That the Healer of my soul be near me;
Give Thou to me, O God,
The death of joy and of peace.

Give Thou to me, O God,
To confess the death of Christ;
Give Thou to me, O God,
To meditate the agony of Christ;
Give Thou to me, O God,
To make warm the love of Christ.

O great God of Heaven,
Draw Thou my soul to Thyself,
That I may make repentance
With a right and a strong heart,
With a heart broken and contrite,
That shall not change nor bend nor yield.

O great God of the angels,
Bring Thou me to the dwelling of peace;
O great God of the angels,
Preserve me from the evil of the fairies;
O great God of the angels,
Bathe me in the bathing of Thy pool.

O great God of grace,
Give Thou to me the strong Spirit of powers;
O great God of grace,
Give Thou to me the Spirit of undying, everlasting,
O great God of grace,
Give Thou to me the loving Spirit of the Lamb.

The New Moon

She of my love is the new moon,
The King of all creatures blessing her;
Be mine a good purpose
Towards each creature of creation.

Holy be each thing
Which she illumines;
Kindly be each deed
Which she reveals.

Be her guidance on land
With all beset ones;
Be her guidance on the sea
With all distressed ones.

May the moon of moons
Be coming through thick clouds
On me and on every mortal
Who is coming through affliction.
May the virgin of my love
Be coming through dense dark clouds
To me and to each one
Who is in tribulation.

May the King of grace
Be helping my hand
Now and for ever
Till my resurrection day.

Sun

The eye of the great God,
The eye of the God of glory,
The eye of the King of hosts,
The eye of the King of the living
    Pouring upon us
      At each time and season,
Pouring upon
    Gently and generously.

      Glory to thee,
      Thou glorious sun.

      Glory to thee, thou sun,
      Face of the God of life.

'Thanks and a plea to Mary'

I thank you, gentle lady,
with gracious heart so mild,
For that good you have done me
With your sweet child.

You are good and sweet and bright,
chosen from all others.
The blessed child your heart's delight,
My Lord Jesus.

Gentle maid, to you I pray
And to your blessed baby,
For shelter, wherein I might stay
And find God's mercy.

Mary, mother, look on me,
with your loving eyes,
Granting rest and bliss to me,
Lady, when I die.

A Medieval English Lyric

Rune Before Prayer

I am bending my knee
In the eye of the Father who created me,
In the eye of the Son who purchased me,
In the eye of the Spirit who cleansed me,
    In friendship and affection.
Through Thine own Anointed One, O God,
Bestow upon us fulness in our need,
    Love towards God,
    The affection of God,
    The smile of God,
    The wisdom of God,
    The grace of God,
    The fear of God,
    And the will of God
To do on the world of the Three,
As angels and saints
Do in heaven;
    Each shade and light,
    Each day and night,
    Each time in kindness,
    Give Thou us Thy Spirit.

On Prayer

The divine life is the pervading Presence of the Holy Spirit in everything . . . He is in us, welling up from the Father and dwelling in us, in the innermost recesses of our hearts, 'more intimate to us even than we are intimate to ourselves' (St. Augustine), and making us inwardly present also to each other, in the same way as the Son and the Father really abide in each other. The Spirit is present in the whole creation, preparing for the final gathering up of all into Christ, the Son. He is present in the core of each being, in the heart of each man, as a ceaseless call and longing, as an unquenchable thirst for this unity and koinonia. In him the elect already possess and enjoy the things-to-come, for all things to come are already present in the eternity of God, and he who possesses the Spirit possesses everything that belongs to the Father and the Son. *Abhishikta Nanda*

PRAYERS FOR PILGRIMS

We commend unto thee, O Lord,
Our souls and our bodies,
Our minds and our thoughts,
Our prayers and our hopes,
Our health and our work,
Our life and our death;
Our parents and brothers and sisters,
Our benefactors and friends,
Our neighbours, our countrymen,
And all Christian folk
This day and always.

Lancelot Andrewes (1555-1626)

God be in my head,
And in my understanding;
God be in mine eyes,
And in my looking;
God be in my mouth,
And in my speaking;
God be in my heart,
And in my thinking;
God be at mine end,
And at my departing.

Sarum Primer (1558)

O King of the Friday
Whose limbs were stretched on the cross,
O Lord who did suffer
The bruises, the wounds, the loss,
We stretch ourselves
Beneath the shield of thy might,
Some fruit from the tree of thy passion
Fall on us this night!

From the Irish

Lord Jesus, Christ,
The world's true sun,
Ever rising, never setting,
Whose life-giving warmth
Engenders, preserves,
Nourishes and gladdens
All things in heaven and on earth:
Shine in my soul, I pray,
Scatter the night of sin,
And the clouds of error.
Blaze within me,
That I may go my way without stumbling,
Taking no part in the shameful deeds
Of those who wander in the dark,
But all my life long
Walking as one native to the light. Amen.

Desiderius Erasmus (1467-1536)

O Lord Jesus Christ, who art the way, the truth, and the life: suffer us not, we pray thee, to stray from thee, who art the way; nor to distrust thee, who art the truth; nor to rest in any other thing than thee, who art the life. Teach us by thy Holy Spirit what to believe, what to do, and wherein to take our rest. We ask it for thy Name's sake.

Erasmus

Be born in us,
Incarnate Love.
Take our flesh and blood,
And give us your humanity;
Take our lives, and give us your vision;
Take our minds,
And give us your pure thought;
Take our feet and set them in your path;
Take our hands,
And fold them in your prayer;
Take our hearts
And give them your will to love.

Caryll Houselander (1901-1954)

O God that art the only hope of the world,
The only refuge for unhappy men,
Abiding in the faithfulness of heaven,
Give me strong succour in this testing place.
O King, protect thy man from utter ruin
Lest the weak faith surrender to the tyrant,
Facing innumerable blows alone.
Remember I am dust, and wind, and shadow,
And life as fleeting as the flower of grass.
But may the eternal mercy which hath shone
From time of old
Rescue thy servant from the jaws of the lion.
Thou who didst come from on high in the cloak of flesh,
Strike down the dragon with that two-edged sword
Whereby our mortal flesh can war with the winds
And beat down strongholds, with our Captain God.

Prayer of the Venerable Bede

Eternal King, grant me true quietness
For thou art rest and quiet without end.
Eternal Light, grant me the abiding light,
And may I live and quicken in thy good.

Angilbert's Prayer

Grant I may so
Thy steps track here below,
That in these masques and shadows I may see
Thy sacred way
And by those hid ascents climb to that day
Which breaks from thee
Who art in all things, though invisibly;
Show me thy peace,
Thy mercy, love and ease.

Henry Vaughan (1621-1659)

Support us, O Lord, all the day long until the shadows lengthen and the evening comes, and the busy world is hushed, the fever of life is over and our work done; then, Lord, in your mercy, grant us safe lodging, a holy rest, and peace at the last; through Christ our Lord. Amen.

(Based on a Sermon of Cardinal Newman)

A Benediction

Go forth upon thy journey, Christian soul!
Go from this world! Go, in the Name of God
The Omnipotent Father, who created thee!
Go, in the Name of Jesus Christ, our Lord,
Son of the living God, Who bled for thee!
Go, in the Name of the Holy Spirit,
Who hath been poured out on thee! Go, in the name
Of Angels and Archangels; in the name
Of Princedoms and of Powers; and in the name
Of Cherubim and Seraphim, go forth.
Go in the name of Patriarchs and Prophets;
And of Apostles and Evangelists,
Of Martyrs and Confessors, in the name
Of holy Monks and Confessors, in the name
Of holy Virgins; and all Saints of God,
Both men and women, go! Go on thy course!
And may thy dwelling be the Holy Mount
Of Sion—through the same, through Christ our Lord.

John Henry Newman.

O God, who hast brought us near to an innumerable company of angels, and to the spirits of just men made perfect: grant us during our pilgrimage to abide in their fellowship, and in our heavenly country to become partakers of their joy; through Jesus Christ our Lord.

William Bright

Into thy hands, O Lord, we commend our spirits, souls, and bodies, for thou hast created and redeemed them, O Lord God Almighty. Guide us and all whom we love this day, and kindle thy light in our hearts, that thy godly knowledge increasing in us more and more, we may always be found to walk and live after thy will and pleasure; through Jesus Christ our Lord.

Be present, O merciful God, and protect us through the silent hours of this night, so that we who are wearied by the changes and chances of this fleeting world may rest upon thine eternal changelessness; through the everlasting Christ our Lord.

Ancient Collects

The Road Ahead

My Lord God,
I have no idea where I am going.
I do not see the road ahead of me.
I cannot know for certain where it will end.
Nor do I really know myself,
and the fact that I think that I am following
your will does not mean that I am actually doing so.
But I believe that the desire to please you
does in fact please you.
And I hope I have that desire in all that I am doing.
I hope that I will never do anything apart from that desire.
And I know that if I do this,
you will lead me by the right road though I
may know nothing about it.
Therefore will I trust you always though I may seem lost
in the shadow of death.
I will not fear, for you are ever with me,
and you will never leave me to face my perils alone.

Thomas Merton

Traveller, there is no road,
the road is made as you go.

Anon.

I am the Way
the Truth and the Life.

John 14: 6

O Father give the spirit power to climb
To the fountain of all light, and be purified.
Break through the mists of earth, the weight of the cloud,
Shine forth in splendour, Thou that art calm weather
And quiet resting place for faithful souls.
To see Thee is the end and the beginning.
Thou carriest us, and Thou dost go before,
Thou art the journey, and the Journey's end.

Boethius.

Eastern Orthodox Pilgrims' Prayers

Troparion

O Christ, who art the way and the truth, send now thy guardian Angel to go with thy servants, as once thou didst send him to Tobias, and for thy glory keep them safe and sound from all harm and evil by the prayers of the Mother of God, O thou who alone lovest mankind.

Kontakion

O Saviour, who didst journey with Luke and Cleopas to Emmaus, journey with thy servants who now prepare to travel, defending them from every evil happening; for thou who alone lovest mankind art Almighty.

Prayer

O Lord Jesus Christ our God, the Way, the Truth, and the Life, who didst will to journey with thy father Joseph and thy most pure Virgin Mother into Egypt and didst go with Luke and Cleopas to Emmaus, we humbly pray thee, Lord most holy, by thy grace to journey with these thy servants. And as to thy servant Tobias thou didst send a guardian Angel to be his guide, so preserve and defend them from every evil assault of their enemy, visible and invisible, disposing them to fulfil thy precepts and keeping them in peace and health and free from cares; grant them successfully to fulfil all their good intention for thy favour and glory. For thine it is to pity and save us, and we ascribe glory to thee, who dwellest with thine Eternal Father and thine all-holy, Gracious, and Life-giving Spirit now and for ever, and unto ages of ages. Amen.

The Jesus Prayer

'O Lord Jesus Christ, Son of God, have mercy upon me, a sinner.'

[This prayer is said by devout Christians at regular intervals during the day and the night and is used by them as the basis of their meditation.]

Gweddi Blwyddyn Etifeddiaeth 1984/85

Dad Nefol,
Diolchwn i Ti am Hen Eglwys ein gwlad,
Am ei Threftadaeth gyfoethog a ffrwythlon.
Trwy nerth Dy Ysbryd Glan,
dyro inni, ni a atolygwn i Ti,
sylfeini cryfach a chadarnach yn
antur y Ffydd ac yng Nghariad Duw.
Wedi ein gwisgo ag Awdurod ac Urddas Crist,
galluoca ni i fod yn oruchwylwyr a gwarchodwyr
teilwng o'n Hetifeddiaeth.
Ymrwymwn ein hunain o'r newydd, O Dduw,
i weithio a'n holl egni er hyrwyddo Undeb dy Eglwys,
er adnewyddiad a defnyddioldeb yr Eglwys yng Nghymru,
a Ffyniant a Iachawdwriaeth Dy Holl Bobl.
Gofynnwn hyn yn Enw'r Drindod Sanctaidd. Amen

(cyf. E. T. Roberts 1984)

Prayer for Heritage Year 1984/85

Heavenly Father
We thank Thee for the Ancient Church of our land;
For its rich and fruitful Heritage.
By the strength of Thy Holy Spirit
impart to us, we beseech Thee
stronger and more powerful foundations in the
adventure of faith and in the love of God.
Clothed in the Authority and Dignity of Christ
enable us to be worthy stewards and guardians
of our Inheritance.
We pledge ourselves anew to work with all our
possible strength for
the promotion of union in Thy Church, O God,
the renewal and usefulness of the Church
and the Health and Salvation of all peoples.
This we ask in the Name of the Blessed Trinity. Amen.

(Griffith Yonge 1406 &
Geraint ap Iorwerth 1984)

Occidentem visitavit Oriens justitiae

Llon ymwelodd Haul cyfiawnder
A'r gorllewin yn ei nerth,
Pan wasgarodd mewn grymuster
Athrawiaethau gau di-werth:

Sanctaidd gorn ein Dafydd gyfion
Chwalodd bob crefyddol haint:
Gwrthwynebodd gred anunion
Trwy resymol Ffydd y Saint.

Felly hael dywalltodd Iesu
Ddyfroedd iachawdwriaeth rad;
Pan oedd Cymru ar lewygu,
Cafodd iechyd a glanhad.

Trwy lân weddi Dewi addfwyn,
Dad y bydoedd, dyro'n rhydd
Ras i'w ganlyn byth heb achwyn
Ac i lynu wrth y Ffydd:

Fel yr haeddom yn y diwedd
Gael ein huno yn ein gwlad,
Gyda Saint y nefol anedd,
A naw urdd yr Engyl mad. Amen

Breviarium Menevense
Cyf. Silas M. Harris

Holl Saint Cymru

Arglwydd, trefni mewn doethineb
Ein tymhorau is y rhod;
Daw i ben dy fythol arfaeth
Er pob newid sydd yn bod:
Ti ddewisaist Wlad y Bryniau,
Ddyddiau tywyll a di-wawr,
I egluro dy fwriadau
Er dy glod a'th Enw mawr.

Hyd ein glannau pell a olchir
O'r gorllewin gan y lli
Yr anfonaist ti o'th gariad
Son am Groesbren Calfari;
Dros yr Eglwys Lân Gatholig
Collwyd chwys a gwaed dy blant,
A disgleirio'n rhol dy arwyr
Y mae enw Dewi Sant.

Parchwn, Arglwydd, goffadwriaeth
Pawb o Seintiau Cymru wen,
Yr Esgobion a'r Offeiriaid
A'r Merthyri hwnt i'r llen:
Dewi, Dyfrig, Deiniol, Teilo—
Dewr y safent tros y gwir,
Bu eu pader, bu eu penyd
Yn sancteiddio erwau'n tir.

Mae dy fwriad yn goroesi
Holl ddamweiniau daear lawr;
Mae dy Eglwys Lân yn aros
Byth yn dyst o'th gariad mawr:
Dyro nerth a gweledigaeth,
Arglwydd, yn dy waith o hyd,
A'th ewyllys di a wneler
Yn yr Eglwys a'r holl fyd. Amen.

Tune: Eglwys Lan, or Bavaria
(Emynau'r Eglwys 219 or 375)
or:
Reged, Emynau'r Eglwys 437

All Saints of Wales

Lord, who in thy perfect wisdom
Times and seasons dost arrange—
Working out thy changeless purpose
In a world of ceaseless change:
Thou didst form our ancient nation
In remote barbaric days,
To unfold in it a purpose
To thy glory and thy praise.

To our shores remote, benighted,
Washed by distant western waves,
Tiding in thy love thou sentest,
Tiding of the Cross that saves.
Men of courage strove and suffered
Here thy holy Church to plant;
Glorious in the roll of heroes
Shines the name of Dewi Sant.

Lord, we hold in veneration
All the Saints our land has known,
Bishops, priests, confessors, martyrs
Standing now around thy throne—
Dewi, Dyfrig, Deiniol, Teilo,—
All the gallant saintly band,
Who of old by prayer and labour
Hallowed all our fatherland.

Still thy ancient purpose standeth
Every change and chance above;
Still thy ancient Church remaineth—
Witness to thy changeless love.
Vision grant us, Lord, and courage
To fulfil the work begun;
In the Church and in the nation
Lord of Lords, thy will be done. Amen.

Bishop Timothy Rees

Old Welsh Hymn—'O fy Iesu Bendigedig'

O fy Iesu Bendigedig,
Unig gwmni f'enaid gwan,
Ymhob adfyd a thrallodion
Dal dy ysbryd llesg i'r lan.
Tra ym teflir yma ac acw
Ar anwadal donnau'r byd
Cymorth rho i ddal fy ngafael
Ynot ti sy'r un o hyd.

Pwyso'r bore ar fy nheulu
Colli rheiny y prynhawn,
Pwyso eilwaith ar gyfeillion
Hwythau'n colli'n fuan iawn.
Pwyso ar hawddfyd, hwnnw'n siglo,
Profi'n fuan newid byd,
Pwyso ar Iesu, dyna gryfder
Sydd yn dal y pwysau i gyd.

Rho fy nhroed y fan a fynnwyf
Ar sigledig bethau'r byd
Ysgwyd mae y tir o danaf
Darnau'n cwympo i lawr o hyd
Ond os caf fy nhroed i sengi
Yn y dymestl fawr a'm chwyth
Ar dragwyddol Graig yr Oesoedd
Dyna fan na syfla byth.

O, my blessed Saviour Jesus,
Only friend of my frail soul,
In the midst of tribulations
Hold my spirit lest it fall;
When I'm cast in all directions
On the world's most fickle waves,
Give me help that I may anchor
To the only hold that saves.

I may lean upon relations
But I'll lose them all anon,
I can turn to lean on friendships
But they likewise soon are gone.
When I lean on ease and comfort
They can never stable be,
But to lean my weight on Jesus
Will support and succour me.

When'er I seek a foothold
On the shaky things around,
My stage is always crumbling
In fragments to the ground;
But if I can find a vantage
In the tempest in its rage
On the'eternal Rock of Ages
That is safe from age to age.

Translation : The Venerable Samuel Jones, Llanllwni
Tune : Dim Ond Iesu

Jerusalem

My cry is for my city
As desert sands I plod,
Jerusalem, my homeland,
The city of my God.
When will my eyelids open,
When will my head find rest,
In thee, my own true city
Jerusalem, the blest?

Grant me the living waters,
The bread of life I creave,
I would be with my Saviour
Who rules that city brave.
Outside the gate I'm knocking,
Lord, open Thou the gate;
The Temple and the Sabbath
Be ever my estate.

While earth remains my dwelling
I wait that morning's light,
When I shall see descending
Jerusalem the bright;
Although the heavens glower,
And dark the clouds may be,
I sing, and trust as ever,
Jerusalem to see.

Though heavy be my hearing,
And though my eyes are weak,
I hear and see in Promise
The city that I seek:
I see the walls of Zion,
I hear the Jubilee,
I scan the Holy City,
Jerusalem I see.

J. Ceiriog Hughes (1832-87)
translated from the Welsh by D. M. Lloyd

PILGRIMS' HYMNS

1 Who would true valour see,
Let him come hither;
One here will constant be,
Come wind, come weather;
There's no discouragement
Shall make him once relent
His first avowed intent
To be a pilgrim.

Whoso beset him round
With dismal stories,
Do but themselves confound;
His strength the more is.
No lion can him fright;
He'll with a giant fight,
But he will have the right
To be a pilgrim.

No goblin nor foul fiend
Can daunt his spirit;
He knows he at the end
Shall life inherit.
Then fancies fly away;
He'll not fear what men say;
He'll labour night and day
To be a pilgrim.

Author J. Bunyan *Tune J. Bunyan A & M R 293*

2 Lead, kindly Light, amid the encircling gloom,
Lead thou me on;
The night is dark, and I am far from home;
Lead thou me on.
Keep thou my feet; I do not ask to see
The distant scene; one step enough for me.

I was not ever thus, nor prayed that thou
Shouldst lead me on;
I loved to choose and see my path; but now
Lead thou me on.
I loved the garish day, and, spite of fears,
Pride ruled my will: remember not past years.

So long thy power hath blest me, sure it still
Will lead me on,
O'er moon and fen, o'er crag and torrent, till
The night is gone,
And with the morn those angel faces smile,
Which I have loved long since, and lost a while.

Author Cardinal J. H. Newman Tune Sandon A & M R 298

3 Guide me, O thou great Redeemer
Pilgrim through this barren land;
I am weak but thou art mighty;
Hold me with thy powerful hand:
Bread of heaven, bread of heaven,
Feed me now and evermore.

Open now the crystal fountain
Whence the healing stream doth flow;
Let the fiery cloudy pillar
Lead me all my journey through:
Strong deliverer, strong deliverer,
Be thou still my strength and shield.

When I tread the verge of Jordan,
Bid my anxious fears subside;
Death of death, and hell's destruction,
Land me safe on Canaan's side:
Songs and praises, songs and praises
I will ever give to thee.

Author W. Williams *Tune Rhondda A & M R 296*

4 Abide with me; fast falls the eventide:
The darkness deepens; Lord, with me abide:
When other helpers fail, and comforts flee,
Help of the helpless, O abide with me.

Swift to its close ebbs out life's little day;
Earth's joys grow dim, its glories pass away;
Change and decay in all around I see;
O thou who changest not, abide with me.

I need thy presence every passing hour;
What but thy grace can foil the tempter's power?
Who like thyself my guide and stay can be?
Through cloud and sunshine, Lord, abide with me.

I fear no foe with thee at hand to bless;
Ills have no weight, and tears no bitterness.
Where is death's sting? Where, grave, thy victory?
I triumph still, if thou abide with me.

Hold thou thy Cross before my closing eyes;
Shine through the gloom, and point me to the skies
Heaven's morning breaks, and earth's vain shadows flee;
In life, in death, O Lord, abide with me.

Author H. F. Lyte *Tune Eventide A & M R 27*

5 God is working his purpose out as year succeeds to year,
God is working his purpose out and the time is drawing near;
Nearer and nearer draws the time, the time that shall surely be,
When the earth shall be filled with the glory of God as the waters cover the sea.

From utmost east to utmost west where'er man's foot hath trod,
By the mouth of many messengers goes forth the voice of God,
'Give ear to me, ye continents, ye isles, give ear to me,
That the earth may be filled with the glory of God as the waters cover the sea'.

March we forth in the strength with the banner of Christ unfurled,
That the light of the glorious Gospel of truth may shine throughout the world.
Fight we the fight with sorrow and sin, to set their captives free,
That the earth may be filled with the glory of God as the waters cover the sea.

All we can do is nothing worth unless God blesses the deed,
Vainly we hope for the harvest-tide till God gives life to the seed;
Yet nearer and nearer draws the time, the time that shall surely be
When the earth shall be filled with the glory of God as the waters cover the sea.

Author A. C. Ainger *Tune Benson A & M R 271*

6 Father, hear the prayer we offer
Not for ease that prayer shall be,
But for strength that we may ever
Live our lives courageously.

Not for ever in green pastures
Do we ask our way to be;
But the steep and rugged pathway
May we tread rejoicingly.

Not for ever by still waters
Would we idly rest and stay;
But would smite the living fountain
From the rocks along our way.

Be our strength in hours of weakness,
In our wanderings be our guide;
Through endeavour, failure, danger,
Father, be thou at our side.

Author Mrs. L. M. Willis *Tune Sussex A & M R 182*

7 Lead us, heavenly Father, lead us
O'er the world's tempestuous sea;
Guard us, guide us, keep us, feed us,
For we have no help but thee;
Yet possessing every blessing,
If our God our Father be.

Saviour, breathe forgiveness o'er us:
All our weakness thou dost know;
Thou didst tread this earth before us,
Thou didst feel its keenest woe;
Lone and dreary, faint and weary,
Through the desert thou didst go.

Spirit of our God, descending,
Fill our hearts with heavenly joy,
Love with every passion blending,
Pleasure that can never cloy:
Thus provided, pardoned, guided,
Nothing can our peace destroy.

Author J. Edmeston *Tune Mannheim A & M R 311*

8 Soldiers of Christ, arise,
And put your armour on,
Strong in the strength which God supplies,
Through his eternal Son;

Strong in the Lord of Hosts
And in his mighty power:
Who in the strength of Jesus trusts
Is more than conqueror.

Stand then in his great might,
With all his strength endued;
And take, to arm you for the fight,
The panoply of God.

From strength to strength go on,
Wrestle and fight and pray;
Tread all the powers of darkness down,
And win the well-fought day;

That, having all things done
And all your conflicts past,
Ye may o'ercome, through Christ alone
And stand entire at last.

Author C. Wesley *Tune St. Ethelwald A & M R 303*

9 O God of Bethel, by whose hand
Thy people still are fed,
Who through this weary pilgrimage
Hast all our fathers led,

Our vows, our prayers, we now present
Before thy throne of grace;
God of our fathers, be the God
Of their succeeding race.

Through each perplexing path of life
Our wandering footsteps guide;
Give us each our daily bread
And raiment fit provide.

O spread thy covering wings around,
Till all our wanderings cease,
And at our Father's loved abode
Our souls arrive in peace

Author P. Doddridge *Tune Martyrdom A & M R 299*

10 Be thou my guardian and my guide,
And hear me when I call;
Let not my slippery footsteps slide,
And hold me lest I fall.

The world, the flesh, and Satan dwell
Around the path I tread;
O save me from the snares of hell,
Thou quickner of the dead.

And if I tempted am to sin,
And outward things are strong,
Do thou, O Lord, keep watch within,
And save my soul from wrong.

Still let me ever watch and pray,
And feel that I am frail;
That if the Tempter cross my way,
Yet he may not prevail.

Author I. Williams *Tune Abridge A & M R 300*

11 'The Kingdom is upon you!'
the voice of Jesus cries,
fulfilling with its message
the wisdom of the wise;
it lightens with fresh insight
the striving human mind,
creating new dimensions
of purpose for mankind.

'God's Kingdom is upon you!'
The message sounds today,
it summons every pilgrim
to take the questing way,
with eyes intent on Jesus,
our leader and our friend,
who trod faith's road before us,
and trod it to the end.

The Kingdom is upon us!
Stirred by the Spirit's breath,
we glory in its freedom
from emptiness and death;
we celebrate its purpose
its mission and its goal,
alive with the conviction
that Christ can make us whole.

Author Robert Willis *Tune Wolvercote*
More Hymns for Today 179

12 Forth in the peace of Christ we go;
Christ to the world with joy we bring;
Christ in our minds, Christ on our lips,
Christ in our hearts, the world's true King.

King of our hearts, Christ makes us Kings;
Kingship with him his servants gain;
with Christ, the Servant-Lord of all,
Christ's world we serve to share Christ's reign,

Priests of the world, Christ sends us forth
this world of time to consecrate,
this world of sin by grace to heal,
Christ's world in Christ to re-create.

Christ's are our lips, his word we speak;
prophets are we whose deeds proclaim
Christ's truth in love, that we may be
Christ in the world, to spread Christ's name.

We are the Church; Christ bids us show
that in his Church all nations find
their hearth and home, where Christ restores
true peace, true love, to all mankind.

Author James Quinn *Tune Duke Street*
More Hymns for Today 125

13 Hills of the north, rejoice;
River and mountain-spring,
Hark to the advent voice;
Valley and lowland, sing:
Though absent long, your Lord is nigh;
He judgement brings and victory.

Isles of the southern seas,
Deep in your coral caves,
Pent be each warring breeze,
Lulled by your restless waves:
He comes to reign with boundless sway
And makes your wastes his great highway.

Lands of the east, awake,
Soon shall your sons be free;
The sleep of ages break,
And rise to liberty.
On your far hills, long cold and grey,
Has dawned the everlasting day.

Shores of the utmost west,
Ye that have waited long,
Unvisisted, unblest,
Break forth to swelling song;
High raise the note, that Jesus died,
Yet lives and reigns, the Crucified.

Shout, while ye journey home;
Songs be in every mouth;
Lo, from the north we come,
From east and west and south,
City of God, the bond are free,
We come to live and reign in thee!

Author C. E. Oakley *Tune Little Cornard A & M R 269*

14 Ride on! ride on in majesty!
Hark! all the tribes Hosanna cry!
O Saviour meek, pursue thy road
With palms and scattered garments strowed.

Ride on! ride on in majesty!
In lowly pomp ride on to die:
O Christ, thy triumphs now begin
O'er captive death and conquered sin.

Ride on! ride on in majesty!
The winged squadrons of the sky
Look down with sad and wondering eyes
To see the approaching Sacrifice.

Ride on! ride on in majesty!
The last and fiercest strife is nigh:
The Father on his sapphire throne
Awaits his own anointed Son.

Ride on! ride on in majesty!
In lowly pomp ride on to die;
Bow thy meek head to mortal pain,
Then take, O God, thy power, and reign.

Author H. H. Milman *Tune St. Drostrane A & M R 99*

15 Let Saints on earth in concert sing
With those whose work is done;
For all the servants of our King
In heaven and earth are one.

One family, we dwell in him,
One Church, above, beneath;
Though now divided by the stream,
The narrow stream of death.

One army of the living God,
To his command we bow:
Part of the host has crossed the flood
And part are crossing now.

E'en now to their eternal home
There pass some spirits blest;
While others to the margin come,
Waiting their call to rest.

Author C. Wesley *Tune Dundee A & M R 272*

16 O happy band of pilgrims
If onward ye will tread
With Jesus as your fellow
To Jesus as your Head!

O happy if ye labour
As Jesus did for men!
O happy if ye hunger
As Jesus hungered then!

The Cross that Jesus carried
He carried as your due:
The Crown that Jesus weareth
He weareth it for you.

The faith by which ye see Him,
The hope in which ye yearn
The love that through all troubles
To him alone will turn.

The trials that beset you,
The sorrows ye endure
The manifold temptations
That death alone can cure.

What are they but his jewels
Of right celestial worth?
What are they but the ladder
Set up to heaven on earth?

O happy band of pilgrims
Look upward to the skies,
Where such a light affliction
Shall win so great a prize.

Author J. M. Neale *Tune Kocher A & M R 289*

17 Forth in thy name, O Lord, I go,
My daily labour to pursue;
Thee, only thee, resolved to know,
In all I think or speak or do.

The task thy wisdom hath assigned
O let me cheerfully fulfil;
In all my works thy presence find,
And prove thy good and perfect will.

Thee may I set at my right hand,
Whose eyes my inmost substance see,
And labour on at thy command,
And offer all my works to thee.

Give me to bear thy easy yoke,
And every moment watch and pray,
And still to things eternal look,
And hasten to thy glorious day.

For thee delightfully employ
Whate'er thy bounteous grace hath given,
And run my course with even joy,
And closely walk with thee to heaven.

Author C. Wesley *Tune Orlando Gibbons, 1583-1625*
A & M R 336

18 Like the sound of many waters
Let the Church's anthems rise
For our father, great Saint David,
Throned above the starlit skies;
As on earth he sang God's glory,
Guided by his Holy Dove,
Still his voice in worship mingles
With angelic songs above.

Still, O Lord, remember David,
All his meekness cries to thee;
Look upon the land he toiled for,
From all evil keep it free;
Here may priests be clothed with justice,
Here may saints of joy partake,
Here may Christ still show his mercy
For his servant David's sake.

David, Guardian of Christ's people,
Shepherd of his flock indeed,
Tending, feeding and protecting,
Watching them in hours of need;
May thy voice in strong entreaty
To the throne of God ascend,
With prevailing intercession
All who seek thine aid befriend.

Thou who once didst tread our valleys,
To our hills didst lift thine eyes,
Still this land of vale and mountain
Thou in heaven dost not despise;
Plead to God that ever in it
May be offered worship due,
Guard the faith that once thou taughtest
Keep us to thy Gospel true.

Honour be to God and blessing,
Lord of endless power and might,
Glorious in his saints we praise him,
Glory to him in the height;

Be eternal adoration
Paid by all the Angel-host,
To the Godhead, high, majestic,
Father, Son and Holy Ghost. Amen.

Tune Hyfrydol E. H. 301

19 We praise thy name all-holy Lord
For him, the beacon light
That shone beside our western sea
Through mists of ancient night.
Who sent to Ireland's fainting church,
New tidings of thy word;
For David, prince of Cambrian saints,
We praise thy name, O Lord.

For all the saintly band whose prayers
Still gird our land about,
Of whom, lest men disdain their praise
The voiceless stones cry out;
Our hills and vales on every hand,
Their names and deeds record:
For these, thy ancient hero-host,
We praise Thee, Holy Lord.

Grant us but half their burning zeal,
But half their iron faith,
But half their charity of heart,
And fortitude to death;
That we, with them, and all thy saints
May in thy truth accord,
And ever in thy holy church,
May praise thee, holy Lord.

A.M.R. 575

20 God is love: his the care,
Tending each, everywhere.
God is love—all is there!
Jesus came to show him,
That mankind might know him:

Chorus:
  Sing aloud, loud, loud,
  Sing aloud, loud, loud,
God is good!
God is truth! God is beauty! Praise him!

None can see God above;
All have here man to love;
Thus may we Godward move,
Finding him in others,
Holding all men brothers:
  Chorus

Jesus lived here for men,
Strove and died, rose again,
Rules our hearts, now as then;
For he came to save us
By the truth he gave us:
  Chorus

To our Lord praise we sing—
Light and life, friend and king,
Coming down love to bring,
Pattern for our duty,
Showing God in beauty:
  Chorus

Songs of Praise: 502 *Melody from Piae Cantiones 1582*
Arranged by Gustav Holst

21 We love the place, O God,
Wherein thine honour dwells;
The joy of thine abode,
All earthly joy excels.

It is the house of prayer,
Wherein thy servants meet;
And thou, O Lord art there
Thy chosen flock to greet.

We love the sacred font;
For there the holy Dove
To pour is ever wont
His blessing from above.

We love thine altar, Lord;
O what on earth so dear?
For there, in faith adored,
We find thy presence near.

We love the word of life,
The word that tells of peace,
Of comfort in the strife,
And joys that never cease.

We love to sing below
For mercies freely given;
But O, we long to know
The triumph-song of heaven.

Lord Jesus, give us grace
On earth to love thee more,
In heaven to see thy face,
And with thy saints adore.

A & M R 242 *Author Bishop H. L. Jenner*
Tune W. Bullock & Sir H. W. Baker

22 For all the Saints who from their labours rest,
Who thee by faith before the world confest,
Thy name, O Jesu, be for ever blest.
Alleluya!

Thou wast their Rock, their Fortress, and their Might;
Thou, Lord, their Captain in the well-fought fight;
Thou in the darkness drear their one true Light.
Alleluya!

O may thy soldiers, faithful, true and bold,
Fight as the Saints who nobly fought of old,
And win, with them, the victor's crown of gold.
Alleluya!

O blest communion! fellowship divine!
We feebly struggle, they in glory shine;
Yet all are one in thee, for all are thine.
Alleluya!

And when the strife is fierce, the warfare long,
Steals on the ear the distant triumph-song,
And hearts are brave again, and arms are strong.
Alleluya!

The golden evening brightens in the west;
Soon, soon to faithful warriors cometh rest:
Sweet is the calm of Paradise the blest.
Alleluya!

But lo! there breaks a yet more glorious day;
The Saints triumphant rise in bright array:
The King of glory passes on his way.
Alleluya!

From earth's wide bounds, from ocean's farthest coast,
Through gates of pearl streams in the countless host,
Singing to Father, Son and Holy Ghost.
Alleluya!

Author Bishop W. W. Howe, 1823-97 — *Tune R. Vaughan Williams E. H. 641*

23 One more step along the world we go;
In the likeness of the saints we grow;
From the old times to the new
Keep us travelling along with you.

Chorus:
And it's from the old we travel to the new,
Keep us travelling along with you.

David was a holy man of God;
Preached the Gospel ev'rywhere he trod;
Travelled far and travelled wide;
Followed Jesus till the day he died.
Chorus

We are heirs to all that David taught;
And we follow as we know we ought.
Jesus—Truth and Life and Way—
Guard us always in our work and play.
Chorus

We are trying to live close to you;
  Make us loyal soldiers, brave and true.
Give us courage, joy and strength
  Throug your Word and in your Sacraments.
    Chorus

Give us faith and zeal as David had.
  May his intercession make us glad.
Help us too your Church to build,
  That your work on earth may be fulfilled.
    Chorus.

Sung to the tune of No. 47
in 'Come and Praise'

By: William Watkins

ACKNOWLEDGEMENTS

The publisher is grateful to the Dean of St. David's, the Very Reverend Gordon MacWilliam, for permission to make drawings in the Cathedral, and to the authors and copyright holders listed below for permission to use the texts credited to them.

Alison Bielski, A. G. Prys-Jones, and Raymond Garlick and Joseph P. Clancy with the Gomer Press, for their own poems and Mr. Clancy's translation of *Psalm to the Creatures* by Gwilym R. Jones.

Mrs. Nell Gwenallt and the Gomer Press for the poems of Gwenallt.

Idris Christopher Bell for H. Idris Bell's translations *I gaze across the distant hills* and *Between the myrtles* from his *The Development of Welsh Poetry* 1936.

The National Council of the Churches of Christ in the USA for extracts from the Revised Standard Version of the Bible, copyrighted 1946, 1952, © 1971, 1973. Church in Wales Publications for use of the Revised Psalter: the Revised Psalter is copyright; extracts are reproduced with permission; and for hymns from *Emynau'r Eglwys.* A. P. Watt Ltd., for extracts from *The Divine Office.* The Administrator of the Shrine of Our Lady at Walsingham for material from the Walsingham Pilgrim's Manual.

Faber and Faber Ltd., for *The Woodland Mass* from *Welsh Poems: Sixth Century to 1600* translated and compiled by Gwyn Williams. Oxford University Press for Gwyn Jones' translation of *Cymru* by D. Gwenallt Jones from *The Oxford Book of Welsh Verse in English;* and for *God is love; his the care* by Percy Dearmer (1867-1936) from *Enlarged Songs of Praise.* Geoffrey Chapman, a division of Cassell Ltd., for *Forth in the peace of Christ we go* © 1969 James Quinn SJ from his *New Hymns for all Seasons.* Routledge and Kegan Paul PLC for *St. Columba's Island Heritage* and *The Hermit* from *A Celtic Miscellany* by Professor K. H. Jackson.

Permission has been sought from copyright holders in all ascertainable cases but apologies are offered for any omissions caused by inadvertence or inability to trace. Such errors, if notified to the publisher, will be put right as soon as possible.

INDEX

of the titles of poems and prayers and of the first lines of poems, prayers and hymns in the second part of the book.

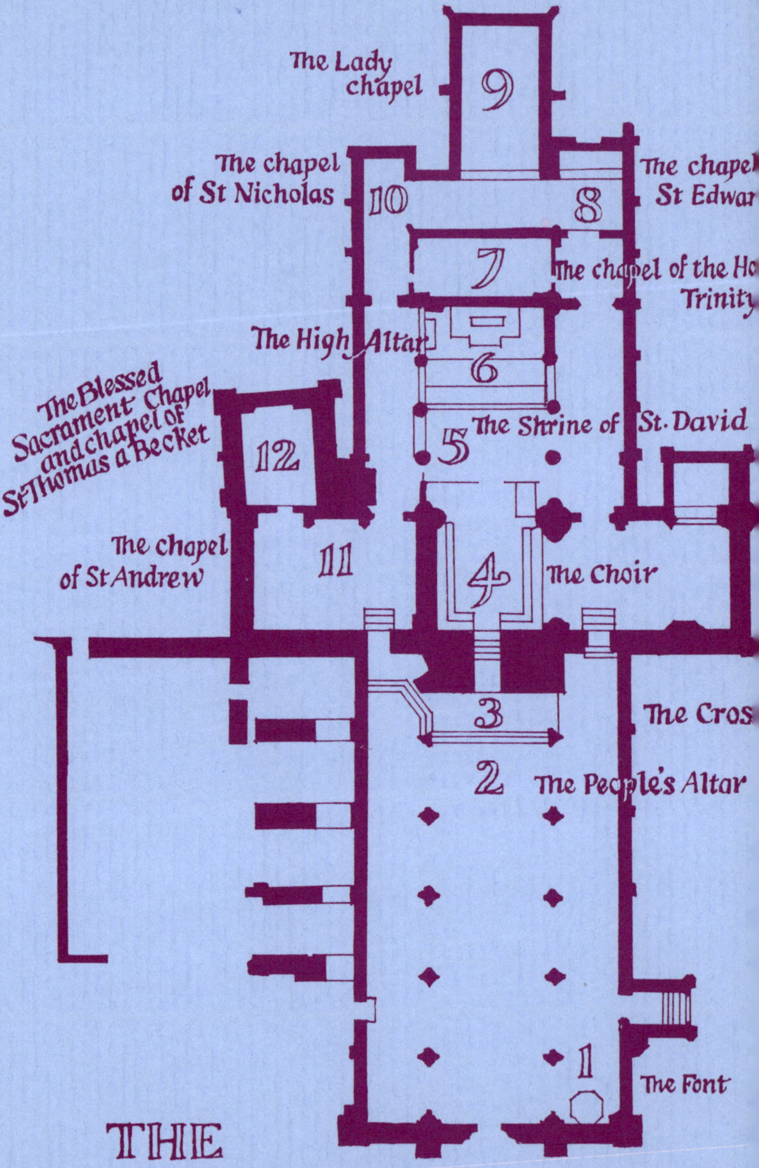

THE CATHEDRAL STATIONS

To go to St. Davids
is much trouble, little profit;
the King of Heaven whom thou seekest there,
unless thou bring him with thee, thou wilt not
find.

Anon.